W0009723

A LOVE AFFAIR WITH MUSIC

The life and times of musician, bandleader and show business icon

GEOFF LOVE

By

Bill Birch

With a Foreword by Norman Newell, OBE

and contributions from

David Jacobs, CBE, Dame Vera Lynn, Max Bygraves, Russ Conway, Sir Ken Dodd, Harry Gold, Ron Goodwin, Barbara Jay, Vic Lewis, Don Lusher, Bill Starling, Tommy Steele and Danny Williams

"A Love Affair With Music"

First Edition

ISBN 978-0-95666701-4

Designed and published by Bill Birch

Cover photograph by Roger Birch, Todmorden Town Hall, April, 1982

Illustrations/photographs scanned to 300dpi
by Daniel Birch, The Woodlands Press, Todmorden, Lancashire

Printed by The Amadeus Press BD19 4TQ

In Appreciation

Todmorden Information Centre wishes to thank Bill Birch and the following individuals, companies and organisations for their financial support towards the book's production.

Stuart and Susan Chadwick – Todmorden

Colin Greenwood – Todmorden

Philip Lord and Carol and Staff at Waterside Care Home – Todmorden

Neil Zechman – Michigan, U.S.A.

Gordon Rigg Garden Centre – Todmorden

Calderdale Small Grants

Team Tod

Todmorden Pride

Todmorden Ward Forum

Foreword

A mutual friend introduced me to Geoff, saying he was an excellent Musical Director. I found listening to his music instantly enjoyable and was greatly impressed with his personality. That coupled with talent are a perfect combination and I started to work with him soon afterwards.

Our association spanned more than 30 years with Geoff becoming one of the most accomplished and sought after Musical Directors in the business. He recorded with many of the world's greatest entertainers including Judy Garland, Marlene Dietrich, Shirley Bassey, Connie Francis, Vera Lynn and Mel Tormé and dozens more top artists too numerous to list here.

In his own right his recording successes included *Geoff Love and his Orchestra; Manuel and his Music of the Mountains; Mandingo; The Geoff Love Banjo Band and The Geoff Love Singers*. He was a huge success on television, especially on the Max Bygraves and Russ Conway series. He became a big star but never forgot his humble beginnings in Todmorden and maintained a lifelong affection for his home town.

I am proud to have been Geoff's producer and, most of all, his friend. I look upon my association with him and his lovely wife Joy who gave him her undying support as one of the most important aspects of my life. I sorely miss him.

As well as looking at Geoff's family history, Bill Birch's devoted research reveals an enthralling account of his life from childhood to the pinnacle of his great career. Those who knew him will be as pleased as I am that this book will ensure it is not forgotten.

Norman Newell
Angmering on Sea
West Sussex
March, 2000

Acknowledgements

In addition to the considerable debt of gratitude already acknowledged to Geoff's sister Connie, Mavis Peach, Margaret Harcourt and Rosalind Love, I must additionally extend special thanks to Norman Newell, Geoff's great friend and producer at *Columbia/EMI* who unhesitatingly agreed to write the book's introduction and contribute notable photographs from his personal archive. Equally, my thanks are extended to the stars of music and showbusiness who provided tributes to Geoff, namely, Dame Vera Lynn, Max Bygraves, Russ Conway, Tommy Steele, Danny Williams, Ken Dodd, Harry Gold, Vic Lewis, Barbara Jay, Don Lusher, David Jacobs, Rod Goodwin and Bill Starling; former *EMI* press relations officer Syd Gillingham, *EMI's* Emma Murray, Janet Lord, Wayne Shevlin, Nigel Reeve and Jackie Bishop. Thanks are also due to Bobbie Mitchell at the *BBC* Photo Library and Michelle Ayloff at the *Radio Times*.

Jane Foster at *Pearson (Thames) Television* was particularly helpful, as were librarians at the *Chicago Historical Society* and the *American Performing Arts Library* in New York City. I must not forget Susan Fagan who was most helpful at the *Newberry Library* in Chicago. Like-wise Cameron Millar at *Warner Music* for granting permission to reproduce significant record sleeves.

I count myself lucky to have met Geoff's former secretary Dorothea Hillier whose recollections, photographs and guidence proved invaluable. Heartfelt thanks also to the following, whose memories and photographs all played their part in documenting his life and career: Todmordians Bryn Allen, William Booth, Percy Dobson, David Evans, Colin Greenwood, Philip Kerr, Jeff Knowles, Albert Marshall, Bob Miles and Dennis O'Neill: Eileen Sutcliffe of Hebden Bridge, West Yorks, Syd Levin, Wilmslow, Cheshire, John Matthews, Billericay, Essex and Reeve Deller of Melbourne, Australia. Margaret Brett and Barbara Price at the *Garston Antiquarian Society* were especially helpful.

I owe special thanks to Sheila Tordoff and John Greenwood at the *Todmorden News* and am grateful to Bill Francis of *Flair Photography*, London, Harry Myers at *PIC Photos Ltd*, London, photographers Chris Hayes of Maidstone, Kent, and Ron Chapman of Winchmore Hill, London, and the *Rochdale Observer* and the *Halifax Courier* for their contributions, as well as the owners of the Carlton Ballroom, Rochdale, where Geoff began his professional career. My gratitude is also extended to Margaret Ferre at the *Crown Copyright Office*, Kaylee Coxall of the *British Phonographic Industry* and to the *Local Studies Library* at Rochdale. Much appreciated was the assistance of *Recordland* and *The Record Album*, Brighton, *Sounds Original*, of Ealing, London, David Mansell of Todmorden for his invaluable help in securing elusive recordings and especially that of Chris Lee, former jazz reviewer of the *Manchester Evening News* and *The Daily Telegraph*.

My daughter Karen is due special praise for her patience and diligence in typing and retyping the ever changing text as is Geoff's mother Frances to whom this book is dedicated. Without her monumental support and obvious wisdom this Love Affair With Music would never have existed.

For Geoff's mother Frances,

who made it all possible;

for his devoted wife, Joy,

and for his friend and

producer, Norman Newell, OBE

Preface

THE market town of Todmorden stands nine miles north east of Rochdale, Lancashire, and twelve miles or so west of Halifax in West Yorkshire. Once, when cotton was king, it was a thriving community where dozens of spinning and weaving mills provided work for most of its then thirty thousand population, whilst music, in one form or other, has been the dominant factor for many of its inhabitants over the last two centuries.

Hundreds of musicians were produced by the town's various brass bands, dance bands and symphony orchestras and during this time more than sixty music instructors lived and taught there. Many of the local musicians became professionals and highly respected in their own particular fields. A few of them were recognised the world over but the most famous of all was unquestionably Geoff Love. Though he died in 1991 he is still idolised and remembered with affection by many in his beloved home town, if not more so by the glittering array of show business personalities with whom he recorded during his exceptional career.

Geoff was a unique person. Though he became musical director and arranger to some of the world's leading entertainers and a prolific recording artist in his own right, his childhood was certainly no bed of roses. He learned the meaning of humility early in life and never forgot it.

On a lifelong show business journey, endearing himself to millions, he could quite easily have crossed his heart in all truth and sincerity and said he really had 'been there, seen it and done it.' That is if he'd wanted to, which is something entirely different. He would have been equally content reminiscing with his first employer Edwin Shawforth about car engines or with his surviving school chums about their back-street cricket and football days as conversing with stars of show business.

Life though, on the face of it, is never what it seems. Before he reached for those stars Geoff faced almost every major obstacle that life could possibly have put before him. Through the ensuing pages readers will learn how he overcame a lot of them, and whilst acknowledgements will be given in due course to those who have contributed to his story, it cannot unfold until special recognition is made of four individuals who were especially helpful.

I am particularly grateful for the information and photographs provided by Mavis Peach of Todmorden and Margaret Harcourt of Sutton-in-Ashfield, Nottinghamshire.

I am deeply indebted to Geoff's sister Connie for sharing with me her special knowledge and memories of her family's formative years and for her permission to publish family photographs.

Rosalind Love has been especially helpful in this direction, providing photographs from Geoff's own collection that were much treasured by his late son Adrian, her husband.

I specially wish to thank band and orchestra leaders Harry Gold, Vic Lewis, Ron Goodwin and Geoff's good friends in showbusiness for the tributes they have extended in his memory. All responded to my overtures, many providing photographs with permission to publish them as well as the accompaning tributes. They co-operated for one simple reason: the magnitude and outcome of Geoff's life was much too important to be left untold. I hope I've fulfilled that expectation.

Now, strike up the band: let's take it. From the top!

Bill Birch,Todmorden, April 2017

Courtesy Roger Birch archive

North Street (Burnley Road) Todmorden c1905 showing market fairground area beneath arches.

"CHICAGO, Chicago, that toddlin' town; you'll love it..." wrote American songwriter Fred Fischer when composing his hit, way back when. Betcha last penny too, on the special place the 'Windy City' still holds in Todmorden folk lore, thanks to a Chicago-born young talented dance artist who won over audiences there at a local fairground concert and, through a series of subsequent events, created a remarkable legacy that stands proudly to the present day. To be more precise, he was Kidd Love, whose second son became one of England's most celebrated and best-loved showbusiness personalities, an orchestral arranger who appeared on television and recorded with many of the world's leading vocalists and who was ultimately conferred as an honorary town citizen of Todmorden.

But let's retrace that journey back to the beginning of what is very much a love story with a difference. Like all good ones it began once upon a time and, in that 'Toddlin' Town'...

Chicago, on the west coast of Lake Michigan and once home to prehistoric Indians, French settlers and Mormons, was just a frontier outpost at the turn of the 19th century. Thirty years on it became a town and a few years later, a city. By 1882 it had become the second largest city in America and that same year, somewhere in all that hustle and bustle, an Afro-American named Richard Love, a hairdresser, married Cornelia Whittaker, a direct descendant of the Cherokee Indian tribe and a devoted Baptist missionary.

She would bear him a son, Thomas Edward, destined to become a juvenile sand-dancing sensation at the Chicago World Fair in 1893. His ability would develop artistically and considerably into a showbusiness career which would one day bring him to England and, through a chance meeting with a local family on the Todmorden market fairground, create musical history of which he could never have dreamed.

First though, the ambitious and determined Thomas earned his spurs with a young troupe of hometown music hall show-openers who became so popular that they were invited to join an American variety show due for a short British tour. On his return home he formed a dancing partnership with a young Chicagoan and starred at theatres and music halls as *Mr Black and Mr White*.

Eventually Thomas decided to go solo and to get his 20-minute-or-so act together adopted the stage name *Kidd Love* and developed an opening song and soft-shoe shuffle routine usually performed to the then hit dance numbers 'Lily of Laguna' and 'Chocolate Eyes'. Another speciality was an intricate forerunner of tap-dancing called Buck and Wing, a pattern of complicated steps wearing wooden soled shoes danced in music syncopation to such tunes as 'Black and White Rag'. 'Tiger Rag' and 'Temptation Rag'. His band orchestrations had all been professionally arranged for his act and were not found easy by musicians. Long rehearsals were common before instrumentalists mastered them to his liking.

The term "tap-dancing" was unheard of until 1905 when dancers started fitting metal plates to the toes and heels of their shoes. Before that they glued on pieces of ebony, hardwood and even coins and, in some cases, used thicker leather soles fitted with hobnails which they ground smooth.

Finally came his sand-dancing showpiece, performed on a sturdy two-sectioned linoleum-covered table surrounded by an archway of coloured electric lights. It was draped in velvet with his name *KIDD LOVE* out front, also in coloured lights. Usually attired in either a lavender or pearl grey suit and another change of shoes, he would sprinkle fine silver sand onto the linoleum and, once dancing, create a slick technique with a sound similar to today's tap. At its climax he would leap from the table and take his bows to lots of applause.

An earlier Afro-American solo dancer had been William Henry Lane, who adopted the stage name *Master Juba*. Born free, he became an important figure in the history of tapdancing and, before the American Civil War, was famous around New York as a champion clog and jig dancer, so much so that some rivals advertised themselves as dancers in the style of Master Juba.

As a teenager, he had likewise joined an American dancing troupe and sailed with them to England for a tour of London music halls. Audiences there were captivated with his brilliance and he stayed on as a solo performer after the troupe returned home. Though his fame soared, he never danced again in America. He died in London in 1852 when he was only 27.

There was a marked difference though between Chicago's hectic lifestyle and the more relaxed scene Kidd had experienced in England earlier. He yearned to try his luck there again, seeing a better future in what he considered a more jovial music-hall circuit with hundreds of towns having two or more theatres, with as many as half a dozen acts changing weekly at each one. So, around 1908, with a new catchy headline, *Kidd Love - The Dancing Masterpiece,* and everything he owned in the world, like *Master Juba* years before, he sailed once more for England.

Courtesy Chicago Historical Society

Clark Street, Chicago, 1896. Birthplace of Geoff's father, Thomas Edward Love (ie Kidd Love).

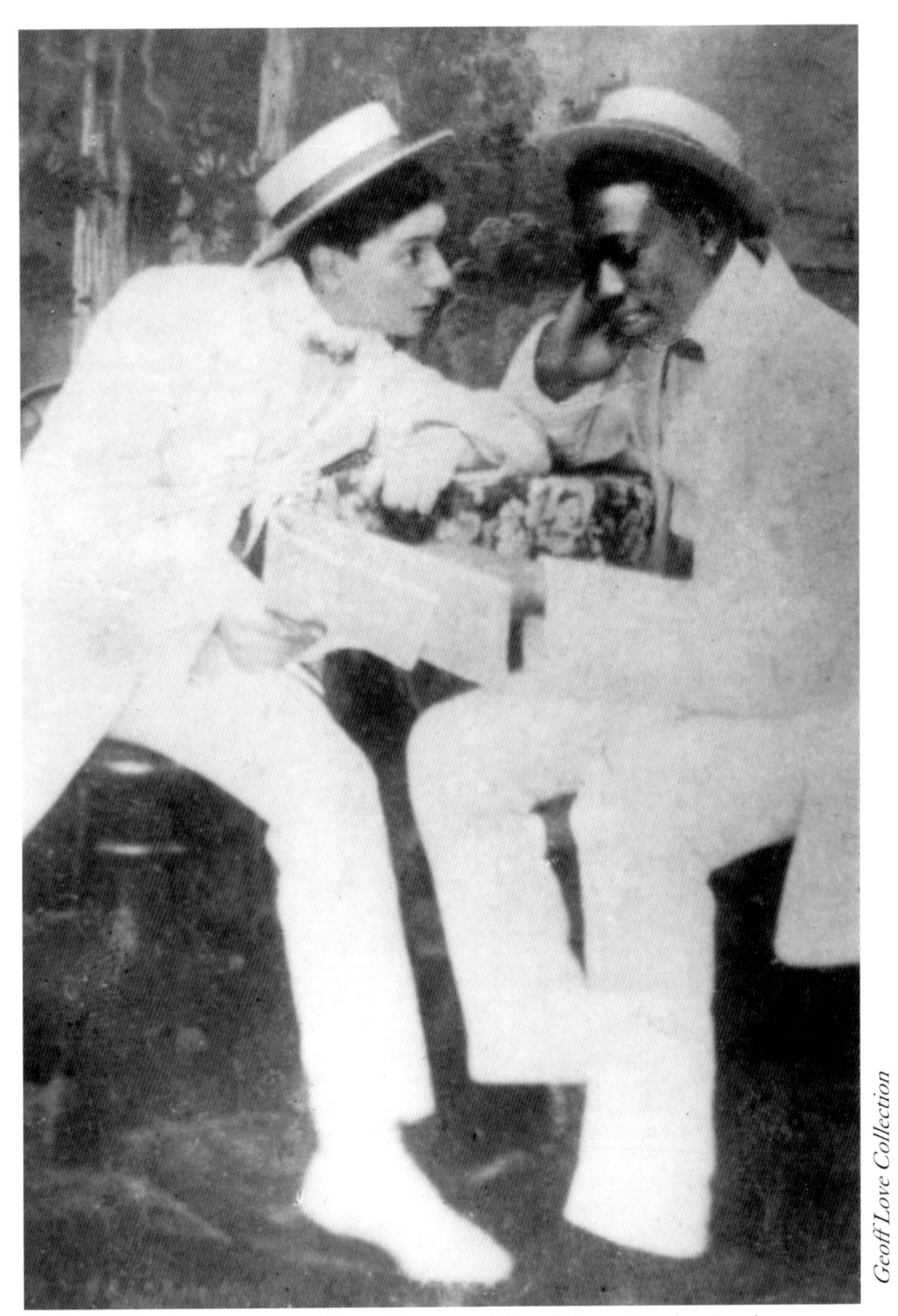

Geoff Love Collection

Geoff's father, Thomas Edward Love, aged 19 at Chicago in a dancing duo, 'Mr Black and Mr White'.

"JUBA," AT VAUXHALL GARDENS.

"JUBA", AT VAUXHALL GARDENS
otherwise William Henry Lane, c1850

(by permission of the
Illustrated London News Picture Library)

circa 1920, when Geoff was aged three.

KIDD LOVE.
The Dancing Masterpiece.

Author's collection

INDEX TO DEATH RECORDS
COOK COUNTY ILLINOIS BUREAU OF VITAL STATISTICS
FROM 1871 TO 1916

PAGE 9,908

---------INDIVIDUALS NAME-----------			--DEATH DATE--			AGE AT		IDENTIFICATION
LAST NAME	FIRST NAME	INITIAL	MONTH	DAY	YEAR	DEATH	DEATH PLACE	NUMBER
LOVE			JUL	11	1911	04 DA	CHICAGO	0000011020
LOVE	ALMIRA		JAN	16	1903	94 YR	CHICAGO	0000009388
LOVE	ARTHUR		JAN	29	1888	06 MO	CHICAGO	0000005983
LOVE	BIRTIE		JUN	28	1889	13 YR	CHICAGO	0000006176
LOVE	BOHUMILA		APR	12	1910	29 YR	CHICAGO	0000010506
LOVE	CAROLINE	E	FEB	13	1899	69 YR	CHICAGO	0000010735
LOVE	CHAS	L	MAR	30	1900	12 YR	CHICAGO	0000010102
LOVE	CLARA		SEP	20	1885	28 YR	CHICAGO	0000069991
LOVE	CLARENCE		JUL	31	1908	21 YR	CHICAGO	0000009903
LOVE	CLEFFY		FEB	20	1886	03 YR	CHICAGO	0000077674
LOVE	CORNELIA	F *	JUN	19	1898	38 YR	CHICAGO	0000011165
LOVE	CUBBIE		JUL	17	1902	03 MO	CHICAGO	0000008768
LOVE	DAVID		APR	30	1911	37 YR	CHICAGO	0000011377
LOVE	EARNEST		APR	27	1892	17 YR	CHICAGO	0000010543
LOVE	EDNA	A	AUG	11	1910	67 YR	CHICAGO	0000010405
LOVE	ELIZABETH		DEC	11	1904	01 YR	CHICAGO	0000009884
LOVE	ELIZABETH	R	JUL	19	1907	86 YR	CHICAGO	0000009323
LOVE	EMELINE		JUN	10	1882	79 YR	CHICAGO	0000005969
LOVE	ERNEST		MAR	04	1915	72 YR	CHICAGO	0000010910
LOVE	ESTA		MAR	27	1913	20 YR	CHICAGO	0000010280
LOVE	ESTHER		DEC	18	1906	60 YR	CHICAGO	0000011568
LOVE	ETHEL	M	OCT	19	1904	24 YR	CHICAGO	0000009733
LOVE	EUGENE		DEC	28	1915	36 YR	CHICAGO	0000011220
LOVE	FRANCES	M	DEC	25	1906	11 MO	COOK COUNTY	0000000433
LOVE	GEORGE		AUG	09	1903	77 YR	CHICAGO	0000009425
LOVE	GEORGE		JAN	18	1898	33 YR	CHICAGO	0000010536
LOVE	GEORGE	C	OCT	27	1880	42 YR	COOK COUNTY	0000000845
LOVE	GEORGE	E	SEP	26	1892	26 YR	CHICAGO	0000010465
LOVE	GUSSIE		JUL	11	1908	27 YR	CHICAGO	0000009910
LOVE	HANNAH		DEC	11	1911	44 YR	CHICAGO	0000011087
LOVE	HARRY	A	JUL	04	1912	34 YR	CHICAGO	0000020066
LOVE	HATTIE	E	DEC	15	1914	53 YR	CHICAGO	0000011070
LOVE	HAZEL		MAR	08	1891	08 MO	CHICAGO	0000009223
LOVE	HENRY		FEB	13	1891	58 YR	CHICAGO	0000009019
LOVE	HERRINGTON		JAN	06	1893	55 YR	CHICAGO	0000010416
LOVE	JAMES		APR	12	1913	76 YR	CHICAGO	0000010451
LOVE	JAMES	H	JAN	30	1913	30 YR	CHICAGO	0000009988
LOVE	JAMES	L	APR	07	1904	34 YR	CHICAGO	0000009782
LOVE	JAMES	M	MAY	15	1902	25 YR	CHICAGO	0000011107
LOVE	JASPER	E	SEP	15	1906	09 MO	CHICAGO	0000009630
LOVE	JENNIE		JAN	15	1882	21 YR	CHICAGO	0000013198
LOVE	JESSIE		APR	30	1883	17 MO	CHICAGO	0000019832
LOVE	JESSIE	A	FEB	20	1897	03 MO	CHICAGO	0000010703
LOVE	JOHANNA		MAR	15	1915	64 YR	CHICAGO	0000010900
LOVE	JOHN		SEP	15	1884	01 MO	COOK COUNTY	0000006685
LOVE	JOHN		DEC	19	1905	90 YR	CHICAGO	0000008210
LOVE	JOHN		MAY	25	1891	36 YR	CHICAGO	0000009601
LOVE	JOHN		AUG	02	1913	03 MO	CHICAGO	0000010485
LOVE	JOHN	A	MAY	31	1915	48 YR	CHICAGO	0000010473
LOVE	JOHN	H	DEC	25	1893	32 YR	CHICAGO	0000011166
LOVE	JOHN	Y	SEP	03	1889	60 YR	CHICAGO	0000006464

A record of the death of Kidd Love's mother Cornelia, taken from official documents held in Chicago. (Died. 19 June, 1898).

Author's Collection

Author's Collection

Birthplace of Geoff's mother, Frances, c1892

Meanwhile in Garston, then a small township of 10,000 or so inhabitants, six miles south of Liverpool and half a mile inland from the River Mersey, a young assistant school teacher and would-be local comedian named Johnson Ambler Maycock lived at 8, Mona Street, with his wife Jane (*née Brown*). Johnson, bearing the middle name of his mother's surname, Frances Ambler, had been born in what is now Accrington, Lancashire, on 15th February, 1871. His father, Thomas, was an artist. Jane was born in Ludlow, Shropshire, on 19th October, 1869; her father, also called Thomas, worked on the railways. They were married at St. Mary's Parish Church, in Rawtenstall, Lancashire, on 24th September, 1888, both declaring their ages as 21, not meeting the then legal requirement. Living at their home at 8, Mona Street, they had four children, naming their first-born, Fred, followed by Gladys, Johnson and Frances Helen, who came into the world on September 27, 1892. While the children were still young their father developed a penchant for acting, became quite good at it and, as is still widespread in the acting profession, adopted a stage name. On the boards he became known as Johnson Harcourt and, with an acting troupe, toured market fairgrounds complete with marquee and portable stage.

Leaning to melodrama, he was soon cutting a dash as *Sweeney Todd* and helped draw the crowds as the villain in *Maria Martin* and other barnstormers of the time. A combination of talent and versatility brought him leading Dickensian roles in *The Old Curiosity Shop* and *A Tale of Two Cities,* in which his daughter, Frances, played a young boy. She also played Little Eva in *Uncle Tom's Cabin*. The tour had stopped at least once in Todmorden and, after Johnson Harcourt and his wife became separated, Mrs Harcourt, as she was known, decided she liked the town well enough to settle there. For a time they lived in the district between Shade and Copperas House, but later settled at 76, Cambridge Street, off Halifax Road.

Kidd Love meanwhile was still building a name working the very same fairground "fit-ups" and another piece of this jigsaw fell into place when his tour arrived at Todmorden one weekend and the 'Harcourt' family went to the market fairground to see the show. Either their paths had crossed somewhere before or Kidd became besotted with Frances there and then; whichever way, he asked for her hand in marriage. It was declined as Frances was under age and she probably thought little of his promise "never to forget her".

Less than two years later Kidd, now 25 years old, had progressed onto the theatre circuit and returned to Todmorden with a week's engagement at the old *Olympia Theatre*, from March 13, 1911. Frances Helen, who had become 19 years of age, went to the theatre, later accepted his second proposal of marriage and with Kidd's audience popularity bringing a return engagement at the *Olympia Theatre* for the week of September 15, they made plans to be married at the Todmorden register office on December 19, 1911.

Kidd's touring schedule became busier than ever with appearances at music halls and theatres all over the country. Frances travelled with him as a complete secretary, booking all engagements and living accommodation until, expecting their first child, she returned to her mother's home at 76, Cambridge Street. Fred Thomas was born there on October 2, 1912, and then on June 3, 1914, a daughter, Cornelia, blessed with the name of Kidd's American mother.

Tragedy struck the family though during July, 1917, when Kidd was appearing at the Queen's Theatre, Peel Street, Farnworth, near Bolton. Only four years old, their son Fred developed acute pneumonia and died on July 14 at their lodgings at 23, Vernon Street. A few days later he was laid to rest at Christ Church, Todmorden.

Frances meanwhile was expecting a third child, a boy, who was born not long afterwards at 76, Cambridge Street. His story became far reaching and he went through most of it with a trademark smile like a Cheshire cat. In truth he was almost born with it as can be seen from a rare early photograph on page 26. They called him Geoffrey — Geoffrey Love.

Author's Collection

CAUTION: There are offences relating to falsifying or altering a certificate and using or possessing a false certificate. ©Crown copyright

CERTIFIED COPY OF AN ENTRY OF MARRIAGE
Pursuant to the Marriage Act 1949

WARNING: A CERTIFICATE IS NOT EVIDENCE OF IDENTITY.

[Printed by the authority of the Registrar General.]

AC 097468

M. Cert.
S.R./R.B.D.

Registration District Haslingden

1888. Marriage solemnized at the Parish Church in the Parish of Rawtenstall in the County of Lancaster

No.	When Married.	Name and Surname.	Age.	Condition.	Rank or Profession.	Residence at the time of Marriage.	Father's Name and Surname.	Rank or Profession of Father.
443	November 24th 1888	Johnson Ambler Maycock	21	Bachelor	Actor	Waterfoot	Claud Maycock deceased	Actor
		Jane Brown	21	Spinster	Drawer	Cloughfold	Thomas Brown deceased	Railway Servant

Married in the Parish Church according to the Rites and Ceremonies of the Established Church, by ______ or after Certificate by me,
J. Morris

This Marriage was solemnized between us, Johnson Ambler Maycock, Jane Brown

in the Presence of us, Joseph Lloyd, Margaret Jane Kirk

Certified to be a true copy of an entry in a register in my custody. J Gregson Deputy Superintendent Registrar 7th September 2012 Date

The marriage certificate of the parents of Geoff's mother Frances, c.24 Nov., 1888

Two views of Mona Street, Garston

Courtesy of Garston Antiquarian Society

Courtesy Roger Birch archive

The Todmorden market fairground c.1890-1910, where travelling troupes of thespians once performed, inside huge marquees.

GUARANTEE SUCCESS EVERYWHERE.

THE DANCING MASTERPIECE.

AWAY FROM ALL OTHER DANCING ACTS.

And Nicely Dressed,
With a Style of my own.

The Famous American
Coloured Artiste and Speciality
Buck, Wing and Sand Dancer.

In a Refined Novelty Act **ELECTRIC ILLUMINATED TABLE.**

OH MY! THAT UNBLEACHED GENTLEMAN. SOME DANCER.

P.A. 76, Cambridge Street, TODMORDEN. Yorks.

This week ....

Next week Monday - Sept. 11th - 1911

OLYMPIA.

NEXT WEEK:
JACK MONKS,
The Premier Tenor of the Halls!!!
KIDD LOVE,
The Renowned Coloured Vocalist and Dancer.
QUEENIE KING, Dainty Comedienne.
MICHAEL MADDEN—"Queen of Dames."
N.C.T. PICTURES.
WEEK NIGHTS, Once Nightly at **7-30.**
SATURDAY—Twice Nightly—7 and 9.
Popular Prices: 3d., 4d., 6d. and 9d.
Children's Matinees—Saturdays at 2-30.
5389 G. JAKOBER. Manager.

Courtesy Connie James

Certified Copy of an Entry of Marriage.

Pursuant to the Births, Deaths, and Marriages Registration Acts 1836 to 1856.

Superintendent Registrar's District of Todmorden

1911. Marriage Solemnized at Register Office, Todmorden in the District of Todmorden in the County of York WR

No.	When Married	Name and Surname.	Age.	Condition.	Rank or Profession.	Residence at the time of Marriage.	Father's Name and Surname.	Rank or Profession of Father.
105	Nineteenth December 1911	Thomas Edward Love	25 years	Bachelor	Music Hall Artiste	18 Jubilee Terrace Tumfield Plain Durham	Richard Love	Hair-dresser
		Frances Hellen Maycock	19 years	Spinster	—	76 Cambridge Street Todmorden	Johnson Aveller Maycock	Actor

Married in the Register Office ~~according to the Rites and Ceremonies of the~~ by Licence before ~~by~~ me,

This Marriage was Solemnized between us, Thomas Edward Love, Frances Hellen Maycock

in the Presence of us, James Gilmartin, Isabella Kaye

Wm Postlethwaite Registrar
Fred. Hollinrake Superintendent Registrar

I, William Postlethwaite Registrar of Marriages for the District of Todmorden in the County of York WR do hereby Certify that this is a True Copy of the Entry No. 105 in the Register Book of Marriages, for the said District, and that such Register Book is now legally in my custody.

Witness my Hand this 19th day of December 1911

Wm Postlethwaite Registrar

The Statutory Fees payable for an ordinary certified copy of an entry in a Register of Births, Deaths, or Marriages, if taken at the time of registration, are 2s. 7d. (including 1d. for the stamp); but if taken at any time afterwards an additional fee of 1s. is chargeable for a search.

The marriage certificate of Geoff's mother and father, c.13 Dec., 1911.

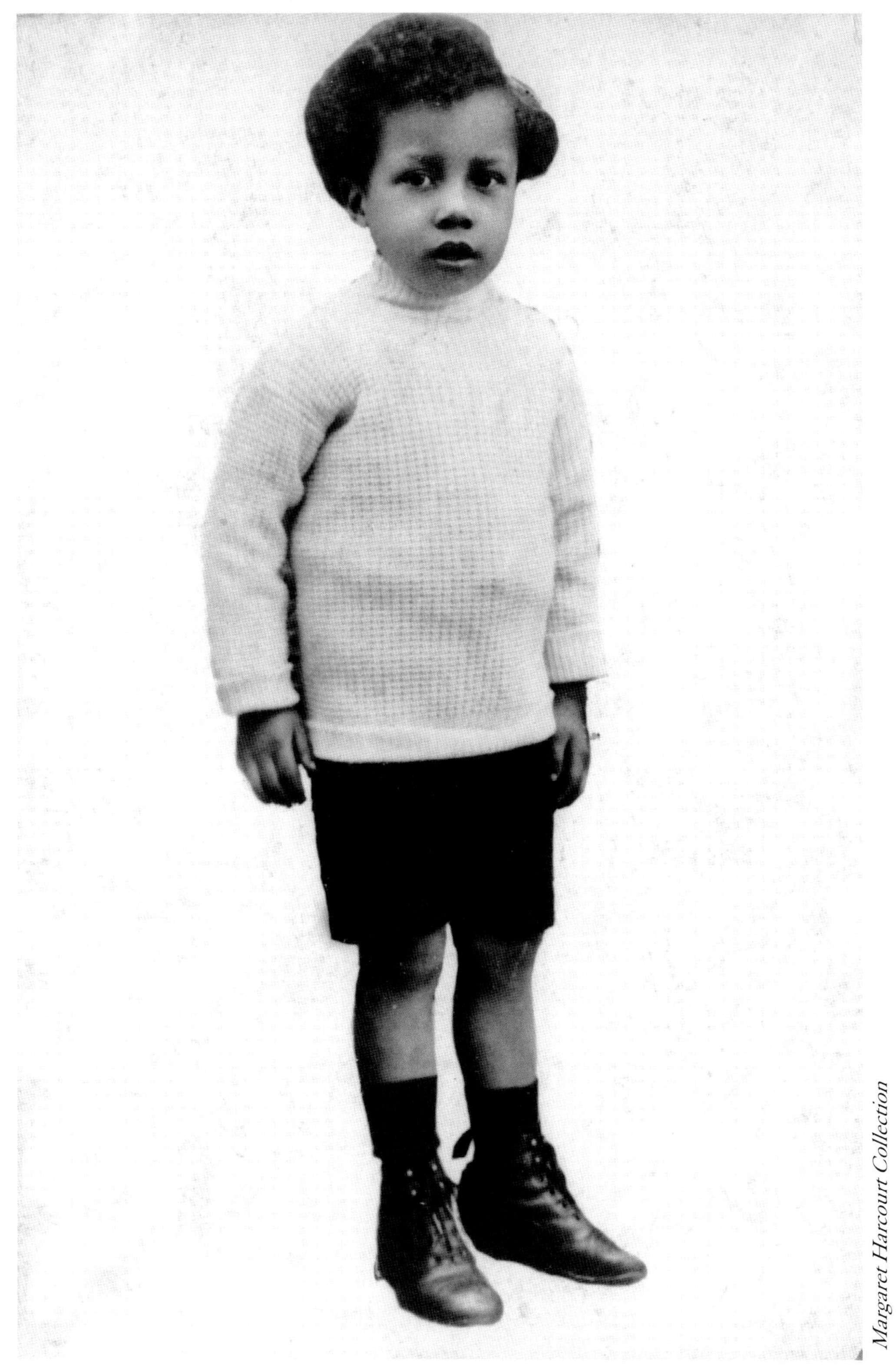

Margaret Harcourt Collection

Geoff's brother, Fred Thomas, born 2nd Oct, 1912, died 14 July, 1917, of pneumonia, less than 3 months prior to Geoff's birth.

[Printed by authority of the Registrar General.]

HC 535508

D. Cert.
S.R.

CERTIFIED COPY of an ENTRY OF DEATH
Pursuant to the Births and Deaths Registration Act 1953

Registration District BOLTON

1917. Death in the Sub-district of Farnworth in the County of Lancaster

Columns:— 1	2	3	4	5	6	7	8	9
No. / When and where died	Name and surname	Sex	Age	Occupation	Cause of death	Signature, description, and residence of informant	When registered	Signature of registrar
185 Fourteenth July 1917 23 Vernon Street Farnworth U.D.	Fred Thomas LOVE	Male	4 years	of 76 Cambridge Street Todmorden U.D. son of Thomas Edward LOVE a Music Hall Artist	(1) Acute Croupous Pneumonia Certified by E. R. Ryner M.B.	Thos. Ed. Love Father In attendance 76 Cambridge Street Todmorden	Fifteenth July 1917	F. Morgan Deputy Registrar Registrar.

Certified to be a true copy of an entry in a register in my custody.

T A Phelan Deputy Superintendent Registrar.
25th November 1998 Date.

CAUTION:—It is an offence to falsify a certificate or to make or knowingly use a false certificate or a copy of a false certificate intending it to be accepted as genuine to the prejudice of any person, or to possess a certificate knowing it to be false without lawful authority.

Death certificate for Fred Love, c.17 July, 1917.

76 Cambridge Street, Todmorden, where Geoff was born, on September 4th, 1917.

Author's Collection

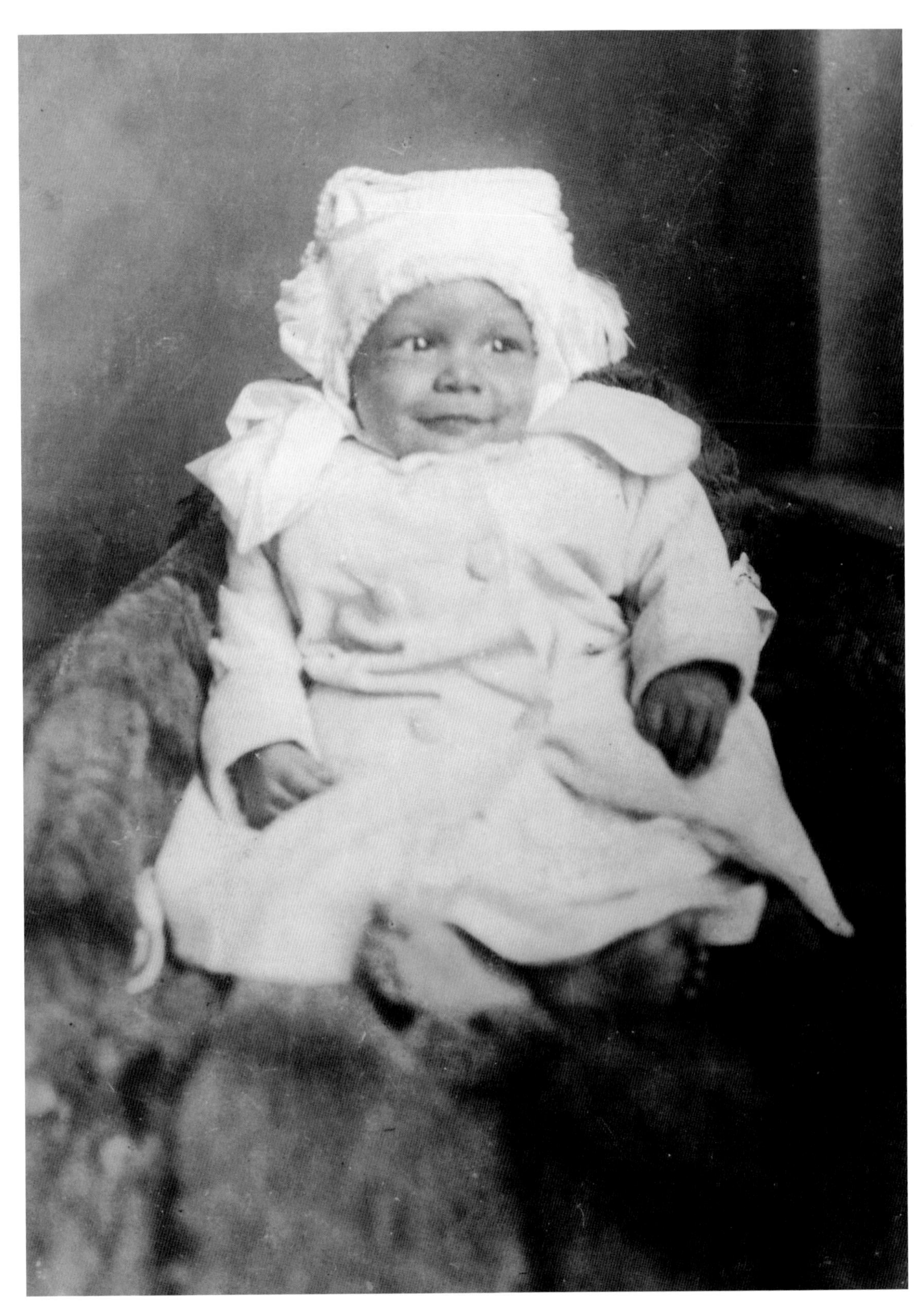

'When you're smiling'… Geoff displays his "trademark" at an early age. c.1918.

Author's collection

Todmorden Co-operative Hall, Sat., 9 January, 1926. Geoff aged eight, as the man-servant in the play 'Susanna's Secret'.

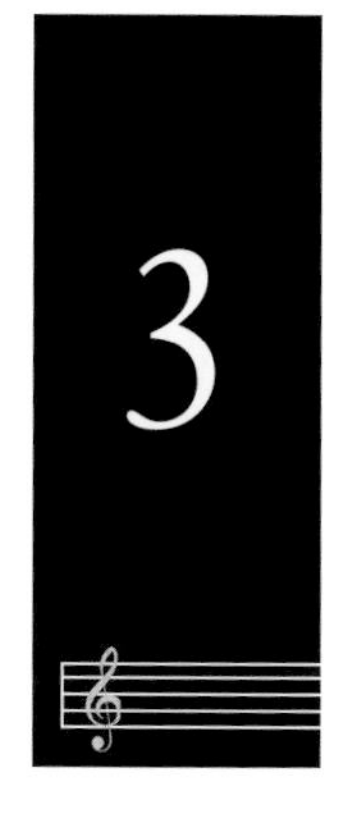

Though his name was appearing regularly on theatre hoardings and his billing position was moving upwards, life on the road for Kidd Love and his young family never stopped on easy street. A typical week would see them spending most of Sunday on trains with all their paraphernalia and belongings loaded into two large skips travelling on to the next curtain call. "Roadies" - road managers - were still some way off so there was all the added responsibility and concern that their skips were still on the train at their destination and needed to be transported to the theatre.

Classed as an alien, Kidd was forced to register his presence at the local police station every Monday morning before he could begin rehearsals for the night's opening performance. Shows were always twice-nightly with matinees midweek and on Saturday; 14 shows in all with the same routine repeated every seven days. Moreover, they could easily be in Scotland one week. South Wales the next and somewhere in Lancashire the week after that.

Kidd's wife, Frances, with daughter Connie and youngest child Geoffrey, who had been born on September 4, 1917, would spend time at the theatre making friends with other theatrical families or meeting up with existing ones with whom they had worked somewhere before. Once the children were five years old though, they became bound by law to attend day school, so their mother's priority every Monday morning was to enrol them for a week at a local school and then at yet another, further on down the line. And so it went on...and on...

At this time Todmorden had two theatres, the original *Olympia* in Burnley Road, awarded its first music and singing licence on March 9, 1911, and the *Hippodrome* Theatre which had opened earlier mid-way down Yorkshire Street on October 5, 1908. Kidd had made three appearances at the *Olympia,* but not one at the *Hippodrome*. Commenting on his third during the week of 20 March, 1914, the local press reported: "The chief place amongst the variety artistes is occupied by Kidd Love who is well known to Todmorden audiences. The nature of his very acceptable turn is his clever dancing with wooden shoes and on the sand mat". Once moving pictures were introduced on the same bill as the entertainers, both theatres were given new titles - *Picture Palace* was added onto *Olympia* and to the *Hippodrome* was added *Electric Palace*. Variety, figuratively speaking, was suddenly no longer the spice of life.

The 20s may well have been "roarin'" in Chicago but stage work in the provinces of Kidd's new life became scarcer. Instead of booking the usual half dozen acts theatres signed up only three and then for only half of the programme. The age of motion pictures had arrived and with it the inevitable road's end for hundreds of stage entertainers whose hopes and dreams were gone forever. Fewer venues made for more and more travelling for Kidd and his family – resulting in less to live on. His wife, calling herself 'Frances May', began appearing in a song and dance act but eventually the strain and stress started to take its toll. Kidd's health suffered and doctors gave him several warnings until, on December 4, 1923, everything ended.

He was appearing at Glasgow in a revue called *Golden Glitter* in which Frances acted as an assistant to an illusionist, Linga Singh, who topped the bill. First Frances would "disappear" inside a cabinet and then later find herself balanced on pointed swords, supposedly in a "trance". Tragedy struck the family once more on the third night of December when Kidd collapsed after the show and was sent straight to Glasgow Royal Infirmary believed suffering from pneumonia. He never recovered and at 2.20 the next morning succumbed to pleurisy and died. He was only 36 years old. His mother had also died young when only 38, in Chicago on June 19th, 1898.

Distraught at their loss, Frances and her two children returned to Todmorden after Kidd's burial in Glasgow and for a time lived with her mother and brother, Johnson, at 76, Cambridge Street. Both Connie and Geoff, as everyone called them, became full-time pupils at Roomfield School and it was not long before both of them showed a keen interest in music. Connie began learning the violin, though her preference had been for the cello. She adapted quickly, so well that she was soon playing her father's difficult band parts, much to the surprise of her tutor, John Bentley.

A number of Geoff's new-found backstreet football and cricket pals were members of Ronald Cunliffe's Boys' Choir and, after a few lessons from the town's award-winning male-voice conductor Harold Lees, Geoff joined the boys choir. At their celebrated concerts at Todmorden Co-operative Hall during December 1925, he played the role of a slave in *The Golden Cockerel* and then a servant in *Susanna's Secret*.

A musical instrument was the thing he longed for most of all and, while given some initial tuition from his sister and her own instructor, showed little interest in becoming the family's second violinist. Instead, watching and listening to the orchestra during Connie's rehearsals and concerts, he yearned to blow the trombone, but the big question remained where it would come from.

Connie James Collection

Connie, with Fred, her uncle, first-born of the Maycock children, and Geoff, not two years old; approx. 1919.

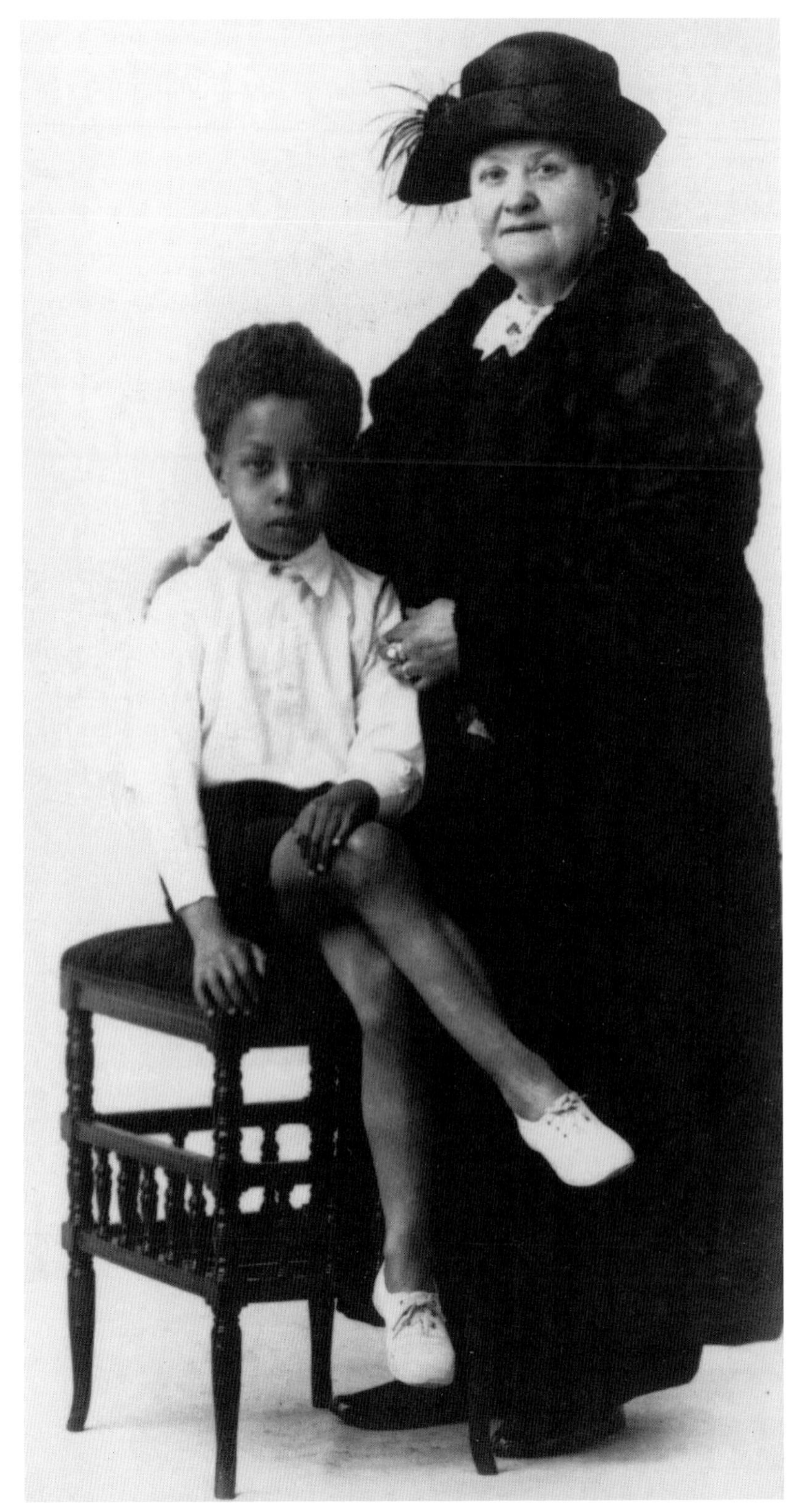

Connie James Collection

Geoff, aged six, with his grandmother Jane.

Courtesy Geoff's sister, Connie.

Geoff's father, Kidd Love, aged 30, with distinctive American-Indian features.

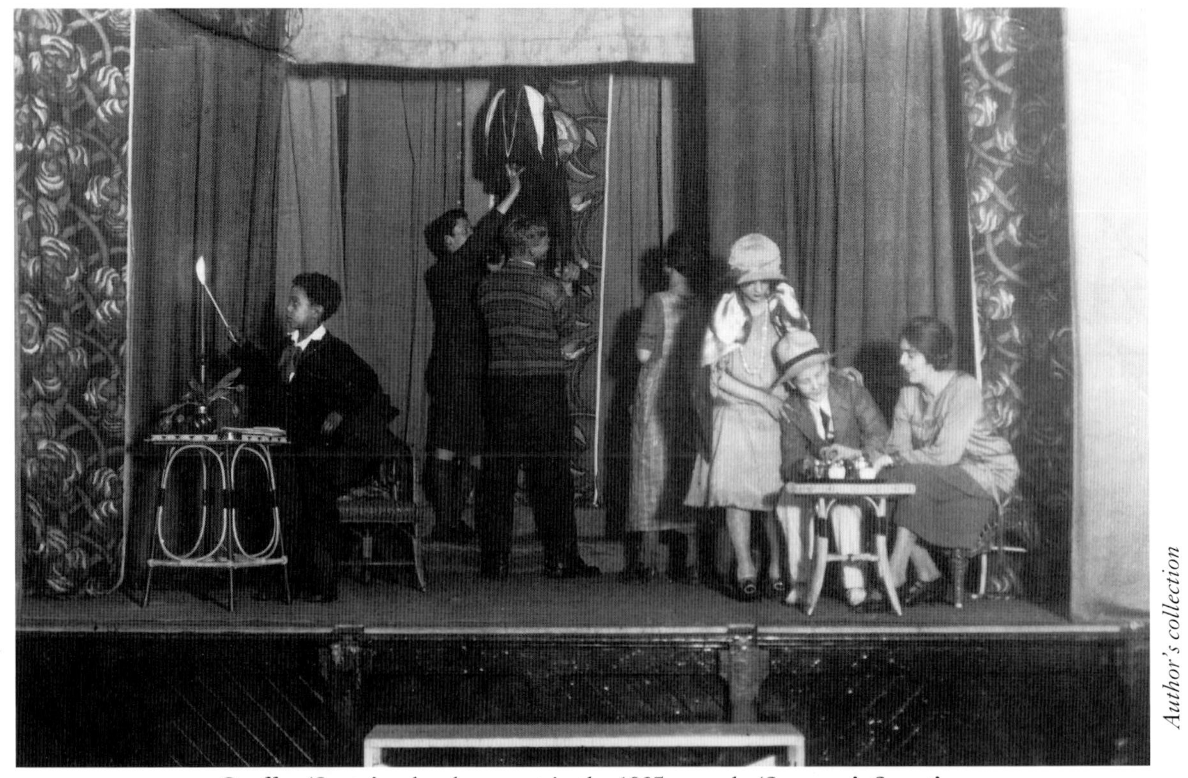

Author's collection

Geoff as 'Sante', a dumb servant in the 1925 comedy, 'Susanna's Secret'.

Author's collection

As a slave in 'The Golden Cockerel' (Pushkin), 1925.

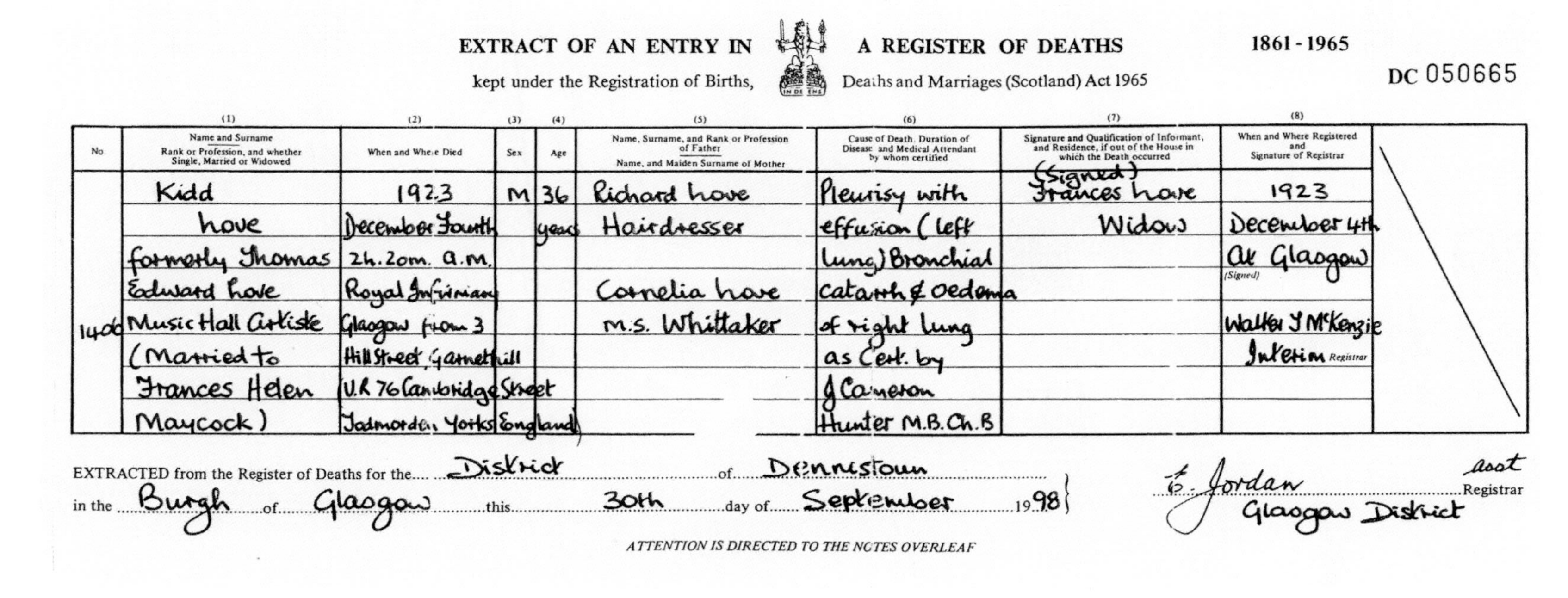

EXTRACT OF AN ENTRY IN A REGISTER OF DEATHS 1861 - 1965

kept under the Registration of Births, Deaths and Marriages (Scotland) Act 1965

DC 050665

No	(1) Name and Surname Rank or Profession, and whether Single, Married or Widowed	(2) When and Where Died	(3) Sex	(4) Age	(5) Name, Surname, and Rank or Profession of Father Name, and Maiden Surname of Mother	(6) Cause of Death, Duration of Disease and Medical Attendant by whom certified	(7) Signature and Qualification of Informant, and Residence, if out of the House in which the Death occurred	(8) When and Where Registered and Signature of Registrar	
	Kidd	1923	M	36	Richard Love	Pleurisy with	(Signed) Frances Love	1923	
	Love	December Fourth		years	Hairdresser	effusion (left	Widow	December 4th	
	formerly Thomas	2h. 20m. a.m.				lung) Bronchial		At Glasgow	
	Edward Love	Royal Infirmary			Cornelia Love	catarrh & Oedema		(Signed)	
1406	Music Hall Artiste	Glasgow from 3			m.s. Whittaker	of right lung		Walter J McKenzie	
	(Married to	Hill Street, Garnethill				as Cert. by		Interim Registrar	
	Frances Helen	U.R. 76 Cambridge Street				J Cameron			
	Maycock)	Todmorden Yorks England				Hunter M.B. Ch.B			

EXTRACTED from the Register of Deaths for the District of Dennistoun in the Burgh of Glasgow this 30th day of September 1998

G. Jordan asst Registrar
Glasgow District

ATTENTION IS DIRECTED TO THE NOTES OVERLEAF

Death certificate of Geoff's father

Connie James collection

The Ronald Cunliffe Boys Choir, photographed in 1925 at the Old Vicarage, Todmorden. Geoff at far right (back row). Choir broadcasted often on BBC radio and performed in several operas before George Bernard Shaw and Vaughan Williams.

Connie James collection

Geoff, aged nine, with his sister, Cornelia.

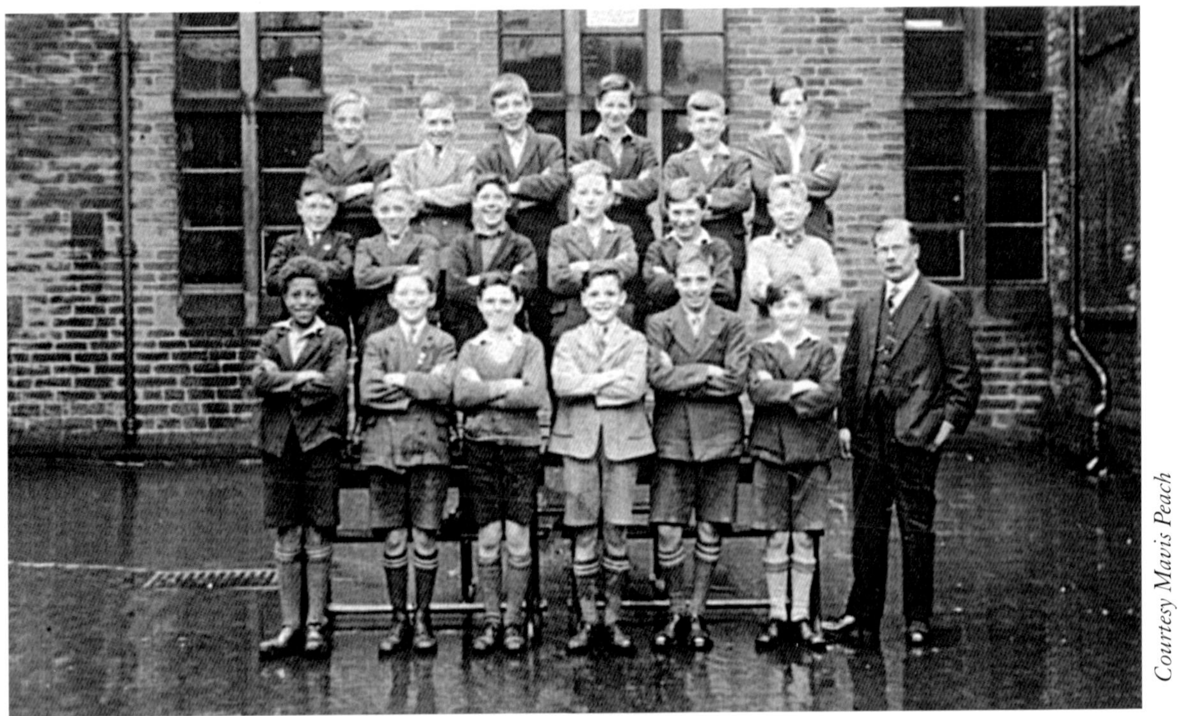

Courtesy Mavis Peach

Geoff – ever smiling – at Roomfield School, aged 11, c1927

Courtesy Mavis Peach

Unitarian Sunday School outing to Great Hucklow, Derbys. c.1930

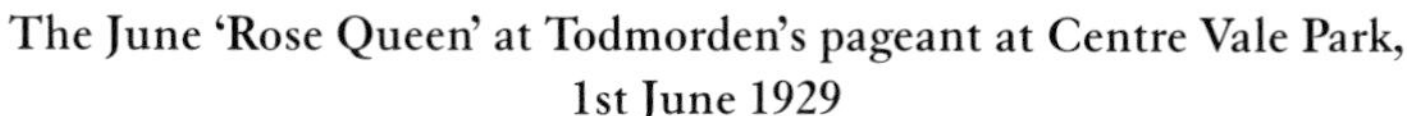

The June 'Rose Queen' at Todmorden's pageant at Centre Vale Park, 1st June 1929

Times were not easy. Frances, working each weekday as a cotton winder at the local Derdale weaving mill, turned her hand in the evenings to dressmaking and general sewing repairs to supplement her income and, much as she wanted to, buying a trombone was beyond her reach. Help was at hand.

The Todmorden orchestra's saviour and anonymous benefactor was its president and prominent town doctor, John de Ville Mather. On numerous occasions he had secretly funded the purchase of replacement instruments and transportation expenses for out-of-town concerts. A skilled trombonist himself, he became the eager Geoffrey's knight in shining armour when loaning him one of his three instruments to start on. His first tutor was orchestra and brass-band trombone player Norris Marshall and, after practising for hours on end, was soon confident enough to join his sister, Connie, in the orchestra ranks. Members of the orchestra were quickly impressed with his apparent natural ability, the president once more happy to fund the cost of a new trombone for its promising young recruit. Frances repaid him though by a shilling each week, a tidy sum in those days. The good doctor, who was studying part-time at the Royal Manchester College of Music, gave Geoff extra tuition, free of charge every Sunday afternoon, after which, and much to his grandmother's delight, he would often return home with a bagful of apples.

On May 31, 1929, the local press announced that Mary Richards, of St Mary's Church Todmorden and its Sunday School, had been chosen as the year's *Rose Queen* for the following weekend's third annual St John Ambulance Brigade two-hour town parade. With a spectacular procession of acrobats, conjurers, ventriloquists, sideshows and the like, its highlight was the Queen's crowning in Centre Vale Park by "12-year-old Geoffrey Love", attired in kilt and tartan.

The previous two Rose Queen festivals had attracted thousands to the picturesque setting, so it was not surprising to see a number of journalists and photographers covering the occasion, with young "Prince" Geoffrey's picture appearing in the next mornings' national *Sunday Dispatch* along with the Rose Queen and her attendants. The pretty Queen of May later trained as a nurse, becoming a leading radiographer at North Manchester Hospital. The youngest of five children in her family, she had two brothers and two sisters. Married in March, 1939, she died in Cornwall in 1975 at the age of 58. She had no children, but adopted two.

In September, 1931, at the age of 14, Geoff left Roomfield School to begin a motor mechanic's apprenticeship at Chew's Garage in Fielden Square close to the town centre, working under the watchful eye of foreman Edwin Shawforth. Not long afterwards, Frances and her two children left 76, Cambridge Street for the last time and moved to live on their own at the old Malt Kiln - now the site of Kilnhurst Avenue - and then, three years later, to their last Todmorden home at 18, Summerfield Road.

By this time he had been in the local orchestra for more than two years and considered himself a capable trombonist. While the town's then leading bandleader, Ellis Wood, believed him lacking as a dance-band musician, another one thought differently. Norman Barker considered him promising and gave Geoff his first "gig", (as musicians call an engagement), with his Imperial Dance Orchestra at the Todmorden Town Hall. Playing in the upstairs balcony, townsfolk watched and listened and were taken with his playing, his effervescent personality and even his vocal touch on a number or two.

By good fortune, midway through his apprenticeship at Chew's Garage, Geoff met Freddy Platt, a travelling salesman for car spare parts, though more importantly for Geoff, a piano-playing leader of a Rochdale semi-pro dance band. Learning of Geoff's keenness and increasing ability on the trombone, and his hopes for a scholarship to the Manchester Royal College of Music, Freddy offered him an audition. Still some weeks short of his 16th birthday, yet easily passing the test, Geoff played a number of gigs with the band and then jumped at the chance to turn pro after Freddy was offered the residency at Rochdale's new Carlton Ballroom.

Opening its doors for the first time on Wednesday, September 19, 1934, the dance hall was considered the most modern and best equipped in the North of England. Coincidentally it had been designed by James Edward Stott, LRIBA, a Todmorden architect in partnership with Jesse Horsfall and Co., and manager of the Todmorden office. His additional hometown credits were the Abraham Ormerod Medical Centre, the Stile Open Air School on the hillside below Whirlaw, Portsmouth Junior School and Todmorden Secondary School at Ferney Lee, later named Todmorden Grammar School. Some time afterwards, he branched out into a partnership in Todmorden with local architect Fred Lindop.

Meanwhile at the Rochdale Carlton, £2 12s 6d for 20-something hours of weekly dance band work was the bottom line for the successful trombone auditionist with Freddy Platt and his Band. Jesse Travis, musical director of Embassy Amusements Ltd, would have the final say and promptly hired the young Todmordian from many applicants after he polished off the test piece as an excellent reader with superb intonation and a laugh and a smile thrown in for good measure. The Love affair with music was about to begin a new chapter - in fact a whole new story. This time its author was Geoffrey Love, and wouldn't he have a tale to tell.

Marget Harcourt collection

At the age of 11, (1928) with his first trombone

Author's collection

'Prince' Geoffrey, aged 11, with the 'Rose Queen's' crown, at Centre Vale Park, Todmorden, 1st June, 1929.

Courtesy Eileen Sutcliffe

Mary Richards, crowned 'Rose Queen' by Geoff,
Centre Vale Park, 1st June, 1929

Connie James collection

Geoff's sister Connie who formed her own school of dancing. c.1937

Connie James collection

The old 'Malt Kiln', Key Sike Lane, home to Frances Love, Connie and Geoff, 1931-1934. Since demolished and replaced by Kilnhurst Avenue.

Author's collection

Norman Barker, born Todmorden, February 21, 1912, gave Geoff his first introduction to the never-ending dance band world in 1932.

Courtesy Mavis Peach

John Chew's garage, where Geoff began his working life as an apprentice mechanic at the age of 14.

Author's collection

Rochdale pianist and bandleader Freddy Platt

Courtesy the Roger Birch archive

The Sobriety Hall, demolished in 1975, was situated at the corner of Rose and Union Streets. Opened in 1851, it was Todmorden's first public hall. Its large function room hosted several local organisations – sporting, religious and musical and became the spiritual home of Todmorden Orchestra for almost a century.

As pay rises go, Geoff Love's first with Freddy Platt's Band in 1935 wasn't to be sneezed at. He'd only been with them three months and already his weekly wage was going up a third - to £4 a week. The bells were ringing.

Like so many aspiring young musicians of his generation, a permanent spot in a resident pro band meant everything. Sure, it was fine to be a semi-pro, on stage playing the 50-50 eight-'till-ones for 3s 6d, or five bob if you were lucky, but this was the *Real McCoy* and what life to him was all about. The Rochdale Carlton, being the North-West's premier dance hall, had professional dancing partners too. Remembering the Rodgers and Hart show tune 'Ten Cents a Dance', Geoff would joke that for a few pennies a dance, a young girl could be twirled into thinking she was as good as Ginger Rogers.

Though a talented pianist in his own right, Freddy Platt had Bob Sharples on piano within his dance band and so, as was the trend, conducted out front. Occasionally, he would feature his new trombone player on a vocal number, and then some nights Geoff would be called out to sing as many as half a dozen. On Mondays, Wednesdays and Thursdays dancing started at 7pm and went on till 11pm and on Tuesdays and on Saturdays until 11.30pm. On Fridays, usually with a full house, the band worked their socks off until 2am and to top it all, two-hour tea dances were held each Wednesday and Friday.

Jan Ralfini led one of the day's popular touring dance bands and just before Easter, 1936, he arrived at the Carlton for a one night stand. Quickly recognising the potential of his opposite number's enterprising trombonist, he offered Geoff a job on the spot and three weeks later he joined Ralfini for a summer tour of south coast resorts. Given that he was barely 19, the ease at which he settled in was remarkable, his fellow musicians immediately taken with his ability and especially his personality. He asked to leave though a year or so later after British Guyana-born Ken "Snake-Hips" Johnson had quietly made him an offer to join his West Indian Dance Orchestra. He was deeply upset when Ralfini refused to release him, but soon brushed the matter aside, stayed on for a couple more years and then took up with Alan Green's Show Band, the main summer attraction of 1939 at Hastings Pier.

He then spent a few months on tour with alto sax player Sid Millward and his Nitwits Band before his call-up in February, 1940, then trained as a bren gunner with the King's Own Royal Rifles. Its Green Jackets' Regimental Band and Dance Orchestra had been over-run by the enemy invasion of France and were forced to disband after most instruments and all of its music library were left behind at the Dunkirk evacuation. When later reforming, Geoff was invited to join the trombone section, became skilled at the art of orchestration and played a large part in rebuilding the dance-band library with many arrangements of his own. Band members were eager to listen to his ideas and always appreciated the tips he gave them.

The regiment was stationed at Winchester and often played for Sunday afternoon concerts at the town's *Ritz* cinema when Geoff was featured as the band's vocalist. As well as singing favourites like 'Shine', 'Chloe', 'St. Louis Blues' and his own composition 'The Ghost of Old Man Mose', he once devised a laughter-packed burlesque pantomime called *Little Red Flying Hood*. In it he gave a clever tap-dancing exhibition, sang the immortal 'Stormy Weather' and could have been 'whistling Dixie' as the audience clapped and cheered his trombone finale in 'Tiger Rag'. Once the war ended, he became a member of the British Band of the Armed European Forces under conductor George Melachrino, touring bases in Germany entertaining troops.

Little of his success could have been accomplished without the sheer devotion of his mother. The law was quite simple in those days about single under 21-year-olds touring around. They couldn't unless chaperoned by a parent or guardian. Though Geoff was then only 16, Frances believed totally in her son's ability and had no hesitation about moving to Rochdale once his future beckoned with Freddy Platt. For the first few weeks he went by train and came home by taxi, but his mother soon changed all that and moved to Rochdale. There she took a different job and went into lodgings with her son at Well i' th' Lane, giving him the chance to devote all his attention to a career she was certain was waiting to blossom.

She went south with him so he could join Jan Ralfini and toured with the band and then, in 1938, when Geoff became 21 and established, decided to live in London and stayed with friends from Hebden Bridge who had a home in St. Margaret's Road, Tottenham, north London. There she worked as a sales assistant in a departmental store before taking greater responsibilities as catering manageress at the *Royal* Ballroom in Tottenham.

In 1935 her daughter Connie, who had started work as a cotton winder at Derdale Mill and later at Mons Mill, Todmorden, married Jim Williams, a local man and head designer at Crossley Carpets, of Dean Clough Mills, Halifax, West Yorkshire, said then to be the world's largest manufacturer of carpets with a staff of 7,000. They lived at 18, Summerfield Road, and Connie, wanting an NATD dancing diploma, began professional tuition at Chorlton-cum-Hardy, Manchester. She busied herself with her orchestra playing, started a school of dancing at the Sobriety Hall in Todmorden and appeared with some of her pupils in variety shows at the Co-operative Hall in Dale Street.

Accompanying the 1936 show was Ronnie Clegg, another local man who made music a professional career. From Castle Hill School he became a pupil of Ronald Cunliffe, a prominent local music teacher and, following experience in dance bands and variety shows, he turned into a sparkling pianist of exceptional talent. After playing in a five-piece band for more than a dozen voyages on the Cunard liner *Queen Elizabeth*, he formed a professional band of his own and also worked in orchestras at leading shows in London's theatreland.

A third tragedy befell the Love family when Connie's husband died suddenly after only four years of marriage. It prompted a move to Tottenham to join her mother where she began advanced dance training, appeared in cabaret and danced in a London revue at the West End's *New Theatre*. Career plans to teach dancing at the Tottenham *Royal* were abruptly scuppered though with the outbreak of the Second World War.

Early, happy days, with Freddy Platt's band, aged 16.

Geoff Love collection

Courtesy the Carlton Ballroom (now demolished)

'Opening Night' – Carlton Ballroom, Rochdale, 19 Sept., 1934.

Courtesy Crown Copyright Office

Atmospheric shot of the exterior, situated off Drake Street, Rochdale.

Author's collection

All aboard to the next gig!

Geoff Love collection

Touring with Jan Ralfini's Orchestra. April 1936-Feb., 1939

Geoff Love collection

Geoff (extreme left) with the Alan Green Orchestra – Hastings Pier, c.1939

A

Souvenir Programme

of a

Variety Concert

in aid of

The Prisoners of War

of

The King's Royal Rifle Corps and The Rifle Brigade.

at

Ritz Cinema Winchester
On Sunday. December 14th, 1941.

Price Threepence.

Geoff Love collection

. . . Programme . . .

Part 1.

⊙

1—**Strike up the Band** ... *Vocalist, T. Edwards*

2—**Rhythm is our Business**... ... *Vocalist, T. Edwards*

3—**You stepped out of a Dream** *Vocalist, A. Wilson*

4—**Johnson Rag** ... ...

5—**Pluckin' on the Golden Harp**... *Vocalist, G. Love*

6—**C'est la Guerre** ... *Vocalists, J Coles & R. Watkins*

7—**St. Louis Blues** ... ... *Vocalist, G Love*

8—**Dead from the Neck up**... ... ... *A. Castle*

9—**Getting Sentimental over You**... *Soloist, B. Teskey*

10—**Blue Skies**... ... ... *Vocalist, T. Edwards*

HOWARD DE COURCEY & "GARBO"
Well known London Cabaret Star.

⊙

Interval.

Part 2.

⊙

11—**Rise and Shine**... ... ...

12—**Wednesday Night Hop** ... ...

13—**Buddy, Can you Spare a Dime ?** ... ...
Vocalist, T. Edwards

14—**The Shot (Melodrama)** ... ...

15—**Danny Boy** ... ... *Vocalist, G. Love*

16—**Tim Lloyd**... ... ...

17—**My Wife has Gone and Left Me** ... ...
Vocals, H. Pratt, J. Talbot, J. Sutcliffe, S. Davies

18—**Two Feet and a Smile** ... ... *G. Love*

19—**Cello Solo** (*Selected*) ... ... *Soloist, J. Sutcliffe*

20 **Night and Day**... ... ...

COMPERE TIM LLOYD.

⊙

God Save The King.

The Green Jackets Orchestra

under the direction of

Mr. A. W. JARVIS. L.R.A.M., A.R.C.M.

T. Edwards, Violin, Vocals.
H. Pratt, Alto Sax, Clarinet.
A. Wilson, Tenor Sax, Clarinet, Violin, Vocals.
S. Davies, Alto Sax, Clarinet, Oboe.
J. Sutcliffe, Tenor Sax, Oboe, Clarinet, Cello.
N. Koedwell, Piano.
A. Castle, Drums, Dancer.

J. Coles, Trumpet.
A. Weinstein, Trumpet.
J. Talbot, Trumpet and Trombone.
G. Love, Vocals, Trombone, Dancer.
B. Teskey, Trombone, Trumpet.
R. Watkins, Bass, Bassoon.
J. Coles and G. Love, Special Orchestrations.

Geoff Love collection

Geoff Love collection

Geoff (extreme left) with the Green Jackets Dance Orchestra. c1941.

Courtesy Mavis Peach

In Royal Green Jackets ceremonial dress. c.1942.

The first of 2 Green Jackets Orchestra concerts as covered by the *Hampshire Chronicle*

DANCE ORCHESTRA CONCERT AT WINCHESTER.

THE GREENJACKETS ENTERTAIN.

A concert of popular music was given at the Ritz Cinema on Sunday afternoon by the Greenjackets' Dance Orchestra (through the kind permission of Colonel R. A. T. Eve) in aid of the prisoners of war of the King's Royal Rifle Corps and the Rifle Brigade, every seat in the theatre was occupied, and the effort raised £88 8s. 9½d. for this most noble cause.

The orchestra was under the direction of Bandmaster A. W. Jarvis, L.R.A.M., A.R.C.M., and the show was compered at extremely short notice by Rifleman Jack François, the popular comedian and dancer, who in civil life appeared in the famous London production, "Funny Side Up," and performed before their Majesties. It is deeply regretted by the organisers that Miss Jane Carr and Miss Marrianne Davies (of stage, screen, and radio fame) and Miss Anne Lenner (of B.B.C. and stage fame, the featured vocalist of Carroll Gibbons and his famous Savoy Hotel orchestra) were unavoidably prevented from appearing at the last moment, but the inclusion of Rifleman François with his cheery personality added much to the great success the show undoubtedly was.

The musical offerings catered for all tastes in popular numbers, and the special arrangements by Rifleman G. Love (trombonist from Syd Millward's band) and Rifleman J. Coles (the trumpeter from Mrs. Jack Hylton's band and Louis Levy's orchestra) were very effective. The rousing "Strike up the band," from the Mickey Rooney-Judy Garland film of that name, opened a most entertaining programme. For modernistic swing fans there was that universal favourite, "Southern Fried," while in sentimental mood were those popular tunes, "We three" (vocal, Rifleman T. Edwards), "Our love affair" (another number from "Strike up the band," with vocal by Rifleman V. Wilson), Jerome Kern's popular ballad, "All the things you are" and Ambrose's signature tune, "When day is done." A medley of Bing Crosby's early hits, including "Where the blue of the night meets the gold of the day," "I'm an old cowhand," "Pennies from heaven," and "Home on the range," with vocals by Rifleman Edwards and Rifleman Wilson, was very well received, as were those tunes in lighter vein, "Down by the old Ohio" and "Johnny Peddler," the popular novelty fox-trot, which featured Rifleman H. Smith (formerly of Ambrose) as the beloved hawker. "Sonia," a trumpet solo, was rendered by Rifleman Coles, and "Danny Boy" was given as a 'cello solo by Rifleman J. Sutcliffe. Rifleman Love was featured in two old and appealing favourites, "Shine" and "Chloe," and also gave a clever tap-dancing exhibition, and devised the laughter-packed burlesque pantomime, in which all joined so wholeheartedly, "Little Red Flying Hood." A fine and much enjoyed show was brought to a close with a superb version of the immortal "Tiger Rag."

The orchestra was made up as follows:—Brass Section: Corpl. Westbrook, Rfn. Coles, Rfn. Weinstien, and Rfn. Love; saxes: Rfn. Smith, Rfn. Pratt, Rfn. Wilson and Rfn. Sutcliffe (also oboe and 'cello); bass violin: Lance-Corpl. Watkins (also bassoon); violinist: Rfn. Edwards; pianist: Rfn. Keedwell; drums: Rfn. Castle.

The second concert, held a short time later, as reported by the *Hampshire Chronicle*

DANCE ORCHESTRA CONCERT AT WINCHESTER.

IN AID OF PRISONERS OF WAR FUND.

The Greenjackets Dance Orchestra—an Army orchestra including players from England's foremost bands now in khaki—gave a most successful concert at the Ritz Cinema on Sunday afternoon, by kind permission of Colonel R. A. T. Eve, in aid of the King's Royal Rifle Corps and Rifle Brigade Prisoners of War Fund. Admission was free, and a collection taken realised £44 0s. 11d. Well before the programme began almost every seat was occupied and hundreds had to be turned away.

The band was under the direction of Bandmaster A. W. Jarvis, L.R.A.M., A.R.C.M., and Lieut. Peter Vokes, of "Band Waggon" fame, proved an amusing and versatile compère.

"Fanfare," the band's signature tune, opened a show of symphonic arrangements of jazz classics, jazz versions of some old favourites, sweet music, popular tunes of the moment, and swing. Rfn. G. Love, the trombone player and tap-dancer, from Syd Millward's Band, was the star of the show, and he and Rfn. J. Coles, the trumpeter from Mrs. Jack Hylton's Band and Louis Levy's Orchestra, were responsible for the outstanding musical arrangements. Rfn. H. Smith (alto saxe and clarinet) used to play with Ambrose.

"Rhythm is our business," the first number, introduced the players and their instruments in turn and provided a rousing start. Rhythm vocals were attended to by Rfn. Love, who led that "hot" number, "Old Man Mo," a jazz version of "Lover come back to me," and a symphonic arrangement of the immortal "Stormy Weather." The rhythmic "Tuxedo Junction" and a jazz version of that dulcet tune, "Sweet lass of Richmond Hill," were also in the programme. Other vocals were by Rfn. T. Edwards, Rfn. A. Wilson, and Rfn. G. Newman. These three formed a trio for that popular present-day tune, "Playmates." On the more sentimental side were that beautiful waltz, "When our dreams grow old" (vocal by Rfn. Wilson), Cole-Porter's romantic rhythm classic, "Begin the Beguine" (vocal by Rfn. G. Newman), "Stardust"—an old favourite with an up-to-date arrangement, "Fools rush in" and "Cuban Romeo" (vocals by Rfn. Edwards). The lighting effects were excellent.

"Lords of the Air"—the tune dedicated to the R.A.F.—heralded by the imitation drone of a 'plane and the flashing of the spotlight as a searchlight, with Rfn. Edwards singing, followed by "God save the King," brought to a conclusion what was undoubtedly the best show of its kind ever staged in Winchester.

This was the first of a series of dances and entertainments to be held during the winter in aid of the Fund. The King's Royal Rifle Corps, Rifle Brigade, and Queen Victoria's Rifles have many prisoners of war in Germany, and by means of the Fund it is hoped to provide the food and comforts which they so urgently need. Gifts of money and clothing for the prisoners of war will be most gratefully received, and a personal parcel office has been opened at the Rifle Depôt.

Courtesy Connie James

Geoff's mother Frances. c.1930/32

Joy as a teenager, unknown location.

One Saturday afternoon during the summer of 1941 while stationed at Winchester, Geoff met Cicily Joyce Peters at the local Lido swimming pool. Born on December 29, 1923, she was the daughter of Cicily and William Henry Peters, headmaster of Hyde Primary School in Winchester. Sitting with friends playing records on a portable wind-up gramophone, she became taken with Geoff's personality and supreme confidence on hearing of his plans to become a dance band leader once the great conflict was over.

After a spell of cinema and dancing dates they were completely in love and while her parents were totally opposed to her marrying a black musician, into what they believed would be a bleak future, the couple were not discouraged and still determined to marry. They did so at Winchester register office at Easter, 1942. 'Wait till you see her', said Geoff to his army buddies, thinking of another marvellous song by Rodgers and Hart.

Harry Gold was another prominent bandleader whose pre-war tours had included the Rochdale Carlton. His Dixieland style "Pieces of Eight" band was known nationwide and often heard broadcasting during the war. In 1943 he needed a trombone player for a series of broadcasts to the West Indies and pulling the right strings was able to "borrow" Geoff from the army to complete them. Geoff joined the band permanently at the Gliderdrome Ballroom, Southend, in July, 1946, and stayed until New Year's Eve, 1949, when he left to freelance. It was a huge loss to them, for the leader considered Geoff a humorous musician of enormous talent, able to play anything at sight and the band's very life and soul.

During his tenure, the Pieces of Eight starred in many popular radio programmes such as Band Parade, Rhythm Roundabout, Variety Concert Hall, Jazz Club, Contrasts in Rhythm and Jazz Matinee. Moreover, in 1947 and 1948, the band was judged the Hit of the Show in the annual all star "Jazz Jamboree" bash at the Gaumont State Theatre in Kilburn, London, in aid of charity.

As well as singing the lyrics on the band's hit record 'BlueRibbon Gal', Geoff provided many of his own music arrangements and wrote two compositions which were soon elevated onto the band's most requested tunes. 'Parade of the Pieces' was an upbeat number used to introduce all the musicians and 'The Ghost of Old Man Mose', a humorous patter song, in unison with the big hits of Tennessee-born singer and bandleader Phil Harris. Harry Gold further encouraged Geoff's talent for orchestrating with commissions in a short-lived agency he ran in partnership with Norrie Paramor.

Geoff was also featured with different bands on the BBC radio's Jazz Club. Produced by Mark White, the show was first broadcast in March, 1947 and became one of the corporation's most successful programmes with Geoff often heard on trombone in an 8-piece band led by Harry's tenor-sax playing brother, Laurie. On guitar was Vic Lewis who ten years or so later, became one of Britain's most popular bandleaders fronting his own 18-piece Stan Kenton-styled orchestra. Occasionally Jazz Club broadcast an all-coloured band assembled from the country's best players including Geoff, with clarinettist Carl Barriteau, double bassist Coleridge Goode, tenor saxist Freddy Grant and drummer Ray Ellington.

Harry Gold

"I saw Geoff for the first time when I was playing tenor sax with Roy Fox's Orchestra. The band did a one-nighter at the Rochdale Carlton, where Geoff played with the house band. It was Freddy Platt's Band and had Bob Sharples on piano. You just couldn't help but take notice of Geoff."

"During the war years I had a contract with the BBC where one of the two lady producers, a West Indian, insisted on the band playing some calypsos in the broadcasts using "authentic players", as she put it."

"At the time one of the band was an army-serving trumpet player, so I asked him if he knew any trombone players capable of playing our style and able to sing calypsos. He said "sure, we have one here in the regiment who would fit the bill nicely". Next thing you know I'm seeing the trombone player from Rochdale!"

"I hired him permanently once the war was over and he stayed with the band nearly four years. Believe me, he was real magic – the audiences loved him. I remember in November, 1948, the band went up to Chelmsford in two cars for a gig at the Corn Exchange. Because of dense fog, it took almost five hours to drive back to town and we only made it because Laurie walked all the way in between the cars with Geoff leading the way with a torch in front of the first".

"In those days musicians of importance eventually formed their own band and I knew within weeks of Geoff joining me that in his case it would become inevitable. He was a natural bandleader who had everything and I was certain he would make it. I'm glad he played in my band."

Vic Lewis

"I first met Geoff in the autumn of 1946 when he joined the BBC's Overseas Jazz Octet for broadcasts on the Light Programme. Later it became known as Jazz Club. At the time Geoff was on trombone with Harry Gold's Band along with Cyril Ellis (trumpet) and Laurie Gold (tenor sax) who were also in the BBC's Jazz Octet. I remember Freddy Gardner played clarinet, Hank Hobson the double bass, Max Abrams on drums and myself on guitar."

"Geoff also supplied the vocals and could certainly swing. Always had a big smile, an easy-going temperament and his extraordinary success wasn't surprising to me at all!"

"We met up again 10 or 12 years later when I was managing Shirley Bassey. She made two or three albums with Geoff and his orchestra for Columbia and I remember being very impressed with Geoff's punchy arrangements. By coincidence about four years later we found ourselves booked at the same hotel in the Canary Islands, and with our wives, had a great holiday together."

Courtesy Harry Gold

Touring with Harry Gold's 'Pieces of Eight', c.1948.

Courtesy Harry Gold

Amazing adulation! Serenading an enthralled ballroom audience with Harry Gold's 'Pieces of Eight'. c1948.

"JAZZ
JAMBOREE
1947"

IN AID OF

THE MUSICIANS' UNION (LONDON BRANCH)

BENEVOLENT FUNDS

AT THE

GAUMONT STATE KILBURN

ON

SUNDAY, 27TH APRIL

NOON

HARRY GOLD
AND HIS
'PIECES OF EIGHT'

Vocalists - - -	JANE LEE GEOFF LOVE
Saxophones - - -	HARRY GOLD LAURIE GOLD
Clarinet - - -	RALPH BRUCE
Trumpet - - -	CYRIL ELLIS
Trombone - - -	GEOFF LOVE
Piano - - - -	NORRIE PARAMOR
Guitar - - - -	BERT WEEDON
Bass - - - -	BILL HAINES
Drums - - - -	ERIC GALLOWAY

Author's collection

Courtesy Harry Gold

With Harry Gold's 'Pieces of Eight', 27 April, 1947, playing the Jazz Jamboree, Gaumont State Theatre, Kilburn, London.

Courtesy Harry Gold

...and once more, at a different venue.

Courtesy Harry Gold

Harry Gold's 'Pieces of Eight' at the Jazz Jamboree, Kilburn, London, 1948.
Left to right: Norrie Paramor, Geoff, Cyril Ellis, Bert Weedon, Harry Gold, Ralph Bruce, Bill Haines, Laurie Gold.

PROGRAMME

ITEMS PRESENTED BY THE PIECES OF EIGHT ARE SELECTED FROM THE FOLLOWING :

HIGH SOCIETY	featuring	The Pieces of Eight.
ON A SLOW BOAT TO CHINA	..	Betty Taylor.
JOSHUA FIT DE BATTLE OB JERICHO	..	Geoff Love.
THERE OUGHT TO BE A SOCIETY	..	The Buccaneers.
WASHINGTON & LEE SWING	..	The Pieces of Eight.
DIXIE	..	Betty Taylor.
THE PREACHER AND THE BEAR	..	Geoff Love.
STARDUST	,,	Freddy Tomasso (Trumpet).
THE JAZZ ME BLUES	,,	The Pieces of Eight.
TEMPTATION	..	Betty Taylor.
THE DARKTOWN POKER CLUB	..	Geoff Love.
WOODY WOODPECKER	,.	The Buccaneers.
CLARINET MARMALADE	..	The Pieces of Eight.
GALWAY BAY	..	Betty Taylor.
I CAN'T DANCE	..	Geoff Love.
BUTTONS AND BOWS	,,	The Pieces of Eight.
THE DREAM OF OLWEN	..	Norrie Paramor (piano)
NATIONAL EMBLEM	..	The Pieces of Eight.
SHORTENIN' BREAD	,,	Geoff Love.
ALEXANDER'S RAG TIME BAND	..	Betty Taylor.
AT THE JAZZ BAND BALL	..	The Pieces of Eight.
LIEBESTRAUME	..	Geoff Love.
HURRY ON DOWN	..	Betty Taylor.
MAN COULD BE A WONDERFUL THING	..	Betty Taylor and The Buccaneers.
TWELFTH STREET RAG	..	The Pieces of Eight.
YOU MADE ME LOVE YOU	,,	Betty Taylor.
HONG KONG BLUES	..	Geoff Love.
MEDLEY OF POPULAR SONGS	,,	Norrie Paramor (piano)
ROYAL GARDEN BLUES	,,	The Pieces of Eight.
EMBRACEABLE YOU	..	Betty Taylor
I LOVE A MYSTERY	,,	Geoff Love.
THERE'S A MAN AT THE DOOR	..	The Buccaneers.
MUSKAT RAMBLE	,,	The Pieces of Eight.
BASIN STREET BLUES	,,	Betty Taylor.
OLD APPLE TREE	,,	Geoff Love.
A FINE BROWN FRAME	,,	Betty Taylor.
THE MAHARAJAH OF MAGADORE	,,	Geoff Love.
VOODOO MOON	,,	Norrie Paramor.
SOMEBODY ELSE NOT ME	,,	Geoff Love.
OLD MAN MOSE	,,	Geoff Love.
DARKTOWN STRUTTERS' BALL	..	Betty Taylor.
THE GHOST OF OLD MAN MOSE	..	Geoff Love.
TIGER RAG	,,	The Pieces of Eight.
SOUTH RAMPART STREET PARADE	,,	The Pieces of Eight.
PARADE OF THE PIECES	,,	The Pieces of Eight.

Courtesy Harry Gold

Left to right: Geoff, Joan Paramor, Norrie Paramor, Peggy Gold, Mr & Mrs Mark White, producer of BBC's Jazz Club, Geoff's wife Joy and Harry Gold. c. late 1940s.

THE MELODY MAKER AND RHYTHM May 17, 1947 THE

The all-coloured band assembled for last Saturday's (10th) "Jazz Club" broadcast was a big success. This special "M.M." picture shows (l. to r.): Dennis Wilson (piano); Mark White (producer); Harry Parry (host-clarinet); Pete Peterson (trumpet); Geoff Love (trombone-vocalist); Billy Munn (secretary-piano); Carl Barriteau (clarinet-vocal); Coleridge Goode (bass); Freddy Grant (tenor); Ray Ellington (drums); Bertie King (alto); Cyril Jones (piano); and Frank Deniz (guitar).

THE MELODY MAKER December 4, 1948

Another "M.M." picture taken during last Saturday's "Jazz Club" broadcast shows (front ow, l. to r.): Cyril Ellis (tpt.); Laurie Gold (tnr.); Freddy Gardner (clart.); Geoff Love (tmb., voc.). Back row: Max Abrams (drs.); Hank Hobson (bass); and Vic Lewis (gtr.). Dennis Neale—drummer on the session with Harry Parry—is sitting behind Hank.

Geoff Love collection

With his great friend Ron Goodwin

Once married, Geoff's young wife became known as Joy, an abbreviation of her middle name, and she lived with Geoff's mother and Connie at the house in Tottenham after Frances's friends had returned to Hebden Bridge to escape the blitz. It was a happy day for all once Geoff was demobbed. He became one of the family and, in 1950, after leaving the Pieces of Eight, he turned freelance doing arranging work for Edward Kassner, teaming up again with his friend Ron Goodwin. For the next three years he either played with or arranged for some of the best known band leaders in the country. They included Ambrose, Teddy Foster, Ted Heath, Cyril Stapleton, Stanley Black, Eric Robinson and Billy Cotton.

Ron Goodwin

"I first met Geoff Love in the mid-1940s when I was working for Harry Gold and Norrie Paramor as a young arranger in the Paramor-Gold Orchestral Service. I occasionally played trumpet with Harry Gold and his Pieces Of Eight and Geoff was the trombone player. He also worked as a free-lance arranger, helping out when the workload of the Orchestral Service demanded it. Geoff and his lovely wife. Joy, would often visit the office with their two little boys, Nigel and Adrian, brightening up the day with their cheerful, happy-go-lucky attitude to life."

"When Norrie became A&R manager at Columbia Records and he and Harry decided to close down the Orchestral Service, I got a job as staff-arranger with the Edward Kassner Music Company, which later became the core company of Bron Associated Publishers. When it became necessary to expand the arranging department, I suggested that we should approach Geoff. He accepted the offer and we soon had a flourishing arranging department, which also included John Gregory, Burnell Whibley, Frank Barber, Harry South and Norman Stevens."

"We worked under a lot of pressure in those days, constantly meeting seemingly impossible deadlines. In spite of this, there was always a wonderful atmosphere in our department, which was largely due to Geoff s carefree manner and our collective sense of humour. We used to take turns at tackling the overnight rush-jobs and I well recall Geoff and Joy popping in when I was burning the midnight oil in our Charing Cross Road office, to drag me out for a drink and a sandwich, in spite of my protestations that I was too busy. Of course, they were right and the work went much better after those forced breaks."

"In 1951 my wife was in hospital giving birth to our son and I was at home in a flat which we had only recently acquired. The doorbell rang and I was confronted by the bailiffs, who had been sent by the Inland Revenue to make an inventory of our belongings, which would be removed if I didn't pay the £80 tax due. I didn't have £80, so I rang Geoff, who readily lent me the money and got me off the hook."

"Eventually, we all went our separate ways, Geoff as musical director to Norman Newell at EMI, while I went to Parlophone with George Martin until my film career with MGM took off. We still kept in touch and in 1982, after Geoff and Bill Starling founded the Young Persons Concert Foundation, they invited me to become a member of the board. Geoff threw himself into this organisation with typical enthusiasm and energy, helping to take orchestral music into schools, where he would conduct all kinds of music, including some of his own arrangements, many of which still form part of the foundation's library today."

"I never saw Geoff lose his temper or upset anyone. His sunny disposition was highly infectious and he made everyone feel welcome in his company. He didn't have to try – it just came naturally."

* * * * * *

Early in 1951 Geoff formed an eight piece band of his own, an impressive line-up that included Benny Green (tenor sax); Harry Klein (alto sax), Cyril Garlick (trumpet), Dill Jones (piano), Don Raine-Young (bass), Cyril Sherman (drums) – later Martin Aston and vocalist Barbara Jay, 19-year-old daughter of Rox Fox trumpeter Tommy Jones. They played for a time at the *Astoria* in London's Charing Cross Road and featured during two summers at the *Regent* Ballroom, Brighton. On September 14, 1951, he took the band to his hometown Todmorden and played to a sell-out all-ticket audience at the Town Hall in support of a Battle of Britain Dance for the Royal Air Force Association. The band cut some sides for the Oriole and Philips labels, issued on 78s, though an upbeat and rhythmic vocal number by Barbara Jay, 'Pretty-Eyed Baby' remained unreleased.

Barbara Jay

I joined the band when I was 19 years old. Geoff was the most considerate person and a very caring boss. Of all the bandleaders that I worked with, he was without doubt the nicest. Also Geoff's wife, Joy, was extremely nice to me and sometimes after the band arrived back in London in the early hours of the morning, making it very difficult for me to get home, she would welcome me into their house and make me most comfortable to stay the night.

"As an illustration how Geoff showed consideration to a young lady vocalist, on one occasion one of the musicians in the band used bad language in front of me. Geoff blew his top and remonstrated with him telling him that while anybody was in the Geoff Love Band they must never swear in front of the lady vocalist. Oh that those values existed today. Nowadays it's often the vocalist who swears at the musicians."

"There were many lovely dates that we did, but one in particular sticks in my mind very clearly and that was the one when we played in his home town Todmorden in September, 1951. The Mayor was there and we were all introduced to him. It was a Battle of Britain Dance for the Royal Air Force Association."

"I foolishly left the band, thinking it was a good move to further my career, but it was a mistake as, with the next two or three bands that I joined, I was never as happy as I was with the Geoff Love Band."

* * * * * *

On radio Geoff was responsible for the hilarious trombone solos with Doctor Crock and his Crackpots – in reality, Harry Hines' Band – and similarly, later with Hal Evans in the *Ignorance is Bliss* series. In 1950 he assembled a 16-piece orchestra and signed with Radio Luxembourg where he was featured in a new series titled *Hello, Young Lovers*. Beginning September 11 it was broadcast at 7.45pm every Saturday with leading stars Joan Regan and Gary Miller supplying the vocal touch.

The personnel of the orchestra was George Taylor, Freddy Clayton (trumpets), Bobby Clarke, Les Carew (trombones), Harry Smith, Derek Collins and Bill Griffiths (saxes), Sid Margo, Jack Greenstone, Bernard Monshin and J. Glazier (violins); David Greenstone (cello); Bert Weedon (guitar), Sid Hadden (piano), Joe Muddel (bass) and Micky Greeve (drums).

The programme became a huge success and showcased many British stars of the day including Alma Cogan, Dickie Valentine, Anne Shelton, Frankie Vaughan, Pearl Carr and Teddy Johnson and pianist Winifred Atwell. In the autumn of 1952 he became musical director for the newly formed Philips label. He was appointed by Norman Newell, who was then the company's recording manager, although Newell departed months later to fill an identical role at EMI-Columbia. Making his recording début with them on November 16th, Geoff went on to form a successful partnership with singer Johnny Brandon, two of their singles making the Hit Parade's top twenty (PB100) and (PB137). He also cut tracks with Glen Mason, namely (PB109) and (PB110) as well as numbers with Jean Carson (PB107) and (PB135) and June Whitfield (PB137). All were produced as 78s as were those Geoff recorded with his own orchestra, (PB117) and, for the Boy Scouts' Association, (Pageant), Parts 1 and 2, (PB151).

He also recorded with Polygon and Polydor until the autumn of 1953, when, with an EMI recording contract in preparation by Norman Newell, he began forming his own studio orchestra from the best jazz and concert musicians in London. The promise he had made to a pretty young girl at the Winchester swimming pool 12 years before hadn't been so brash after all. His star was beginning to rise.

Geoff Love collection/photo Chris Hayes

Own band publicity photograph. c1951

Courtesy Chris Hayes

Geoff fronts members of his first band. Left to right; Cyril Garlick (trumpet), Dill Jones (piano), Barbara Jay (vocals), Don Raine-Young (bass), Harry Klein (alto/bari), Benny Green (tenor), Martin Aston (drums). c.1951.

TO-NIGHT

ROYAL AIR FORCES ASSOCIATION
(Regd. under War Charities Act, 1940)
Todmorden and Hebden Bridge Branch
Present SIXTH ANNUAL

Battle of Britain DANCE

TOWN HALL, TODMORDEN,
14th SEPTEMBER, 1951
DANCING 8 till 2 to two Bands

Geoff. Love and His Music

Featuring BARBARA JAY,
Supported by the Ray Arnold Quartet.

Bar and Buffet. ADMISSION 7/6

CURRENT HITS

IT'S THE TALK OF THE TOWN S.O. 3/-
TOOTLE LOO-SIANA S.O. 3/-
RHAPSODY RAG
8-PIECE DIXIELAND ARRANGEMENT BY GEOFF LOVE 3/-

Harry Gold **"PIECES OF EIGHT"** Series

- ALLIGATOR CRAWL
- AMERICAN PATROL
- CHRISTOPHER COLUMBUS
- DEEP HENDERSON
- FOUR OR FIVE TIMES
- HAWAIIAN WAR CHANT
- SHIM-ME-SHA WOBBLE
- VIPERS DRAG

Eight piece arrangements fully cued. Sets 3/- each

KEITH PROWSE & Co. Ltd.
42-43 POLAND ST., LONDON, W.1 GER 9000

Geoff Love 8-piece for Astoria and Regent

TROMBONE star Geoff Love (*inset*), who formed his own outfit when he left Harry Gold's "Pieces of Eight," gets his biggest bandleading break during the next two months. He is to deputise during the summer holidays at the Astoria, Charing Cross-road, and the Regent, Brighton.

Leading the eight-piece with which he has been gigging and playing Sunday concerts for several months, Geoff will play at the Astoria from July 22 to August 4, while Jack White and his Band are away, and from August 26 to September 8 while Harry Leader and his Band have their vacation.

Geoff goes to Brighton for three weeks, starting August 5, while Syd Dean and his Band and the supporting "Strings in Rhythm" Orchestra are away.

Geoff was with Harry Gold for three and a half years and has since free-lanced both as an instrumentalist-vocalist and as a bandleader. At the Astoria and the Regent he will, naturally, feature Dixieland, but will also play the other styles of dance music to which the parons of these ballrooms are accustomed.

His line-up will be: Geoff Love (ldr., tmb., vcl.), Cyril Garlick (tpt.), Harry Klein (alto), Benny Green (tnr.), Dill Jones (pno.), Don Raine-Young (bass), Cyril Sherman (drs.), and Barbara Jay (vcl.).

Barbara Jay is the 19-year-old daughter of trumpet-player Tommy Jones, who has played for Roy Fox, Timmy Finnigan, etc., and is at present working in Jersey.

Barbara's only previous professional experience has been a few weeks with Teddy Foster.

Courtesy Royal Pavilion Library, Brighton

The Regent Ballroom, Brighton, where Geoff and his first dance band played during the 1951 summer season.

Recordings of Geoff's first
8-piece orchestra

First Published 1957.

Courtesy of Parlophone Records Limited

8

Geoff signed his contract as musical director for EMI in January, 1954, and the same year recorded hit singles with Frankie Vaughan, ('Happy Days And Lonely Nights'; 'My Son, My Son') and five more during the 60s; namely 'Music To Watch Girls By', 'Mame', 'If I Didn't Care', 'Girl Talk' and 'The Best Is Yet To Come', Alma Cogan, ('Do, Do, Do, Do Do It Again', a bouncy duet with Frankie Vaughan) 'Forces Sweetheart' Anne Shelton ('Teach Me Tonight', 'Juke Box Rag") and in 1955 with Max Bygraves ('Meet Me On The Corner'; HMV POP 116). They all became lifelong friends and, along with many other showbusiness personalities, were sometimes seen on Geoff's own weekly ITV series *On The Town*, that started in 1955. Originally planned for just seven weeks, it ran for 54.

Having changed his name during the 1940s from Harold Leek and become a major star of stage and Hollywood musicals, Howard Keel recorded with Geoff during the '50s, 'Love, Wonderful Love' / 'Parisienne'; (Columbia DB3969) and so did the Deep River Boys, a five-strong American gospel-singing group. The numbers they recorded with Geoff were somewhat different though and more in keeping with current trends. HMV released 'Shake, Rattle and Roll' / 'St. Louis Blues' as a 7" single (HMV B10790) and likewise, 'Smack Dab in the Middle' / 'I Wonder' (HMV B10902).

The approaching Swinging Sixties saw Geoff established at EMI/Columbia with a long-term contract, four long playing albums under his own name selling well in the shops and recording sessions with Shirley Bassey and Russ Conway, from whom the company had big expectations. His stature was escalating by the week in a career which his heart had been set on since childhood. Happiness was just a thing called Geoff and most of those associated with him became infected - yet he never forgot where it all started. His former Todmorden Orchestra colleagues and school chums held him in the highest esteem, nor did he ever lose touch with his first employer at Chew's Garage, Edwin Shawforth. His grandmother though, to whom he had been devoted, had moved from the house on Cambridge Street to Sun Vale Avenue, two miles away in Walsden. She died there on 23rd June, 1949, at the age of 79.

Geoff's first three albums for Columbia emphasised his arranging skills for large string orchestras, all of them critically acclaimed. The first one, entitled *Enchanted Evenings* (33SX1060) and first published in 1956, consisted of 14 famous melodies associated with some of the greatest shows ever produced at the Theatre Royal, Drury Lane. The next, released just months later and called *Our Very Own* (33 SX1069), showcased 14 memorable tunes composed by Victor Young. Midway through 1958, Geoff was hailed a musical genius on the release of his third, *Thanks For The Memories* (SCX3257) when A and R manager (Artists and Repertoire) Norman Newell added that the magnitude of his ability had no bounds and that his work rate, by any standards, was astonishing.

Through starring roles in countless feature films and dozens of top-selling albums and still only 37 years old, Judy Garland was already a show business legend when she arrived in London for a month-long engagement at the Dominion Theatre, beginning 16 October, 1957. At 6.30pm on Friday 11 October, she arrived at Abbey Road studios accompanied by her American musical director, Gordon Jenkins, to record a commemorative 45rpm single for Capitol Records that was given out as a complimentary souvenir at the gala premiere.

Geoff assembled his concert orchestra in Studio 2 to record just one song, appropriately titled, 'It's Lovely To Be Back In London', (the first was a four-week run at the London Palladium drawing huge audiences from 9 April, 1951). The single was later issued for general release (45-LC-14791) though the original, with its impressive sleeve, became a sought-after collectors' item. On the reverse side Judy sings 'By Myself', a ballad with a beat, with Gordon Jenkins conducting the orchestra.

Geoff's popularity soared to new heights in November, 1957, after Parlophone issued a single by a relatively unknown London schoolboy named Laurie London. Entitled 'He's Got The Whole World In His Hands' (R.4359) and devised by Geoff from a simple gospel song into a hand-clapping spiritual number backed by his orchestra and the Rita Williams Singers, the transformation almost made the Hit Parade's top ten and stayed in the charts for three months. It was well on the way toward the million mark before Ed Sullivan's nationwide U.S. TV show gave huge American and Canadian audiences their first look at the amazing youngster. When released in the US by Capitol Records (EAP 1-10182), sales exceeded a million and though missing top spot, remained second in the charts there for several weeks. Some months earlier Parlophone had released an album called *Six-Five-Special*, based on the hugely successful BBC Television series, recorded with many of the original artists. (PMC 1047). It was supervised by Norman Newell and featured Geoff with his orchestra accompanying Laurie London on 'Pick a Bale of Cotton' and 'Up Above My Head I Hear Music In The Air'.

Geoff recorded 10 more numbers with him during the next 12 months, all put out by Parlophone as 45s.

Titles	Record number
Boomerang The gospel train	45-R-4408
A railroadin' man I gotta robe	45-R-4426
The Darktown strutters ball My mother	45-R-4447
Basin Street blues Joshua	45-R-4450
3 O'clock Up above my head	45-R-4499

Following a cavalcade of TV appearances and regular spots in London's clubland the King Brothers were considered Britain's best vocal group during the late 1950s. Geoff became their musical director once they signed with Parlophone Records in 1957, making their first single with the label, 'A White Sport Coat' (R 4310) an instant hit. The Marty Robbins number, in the charts for more than three months, was followed by a string of others like 'Wake Up Little Suzie', '76 Trombones', 'Thank Heaven For Little Girls' and the most successful of all, 'Standing On The Corner' (R 4639). The same year, they recorded a tribute to Al Jolson with four of the great artist's most popular songs, released as an EP (GEP 8651): 'I'm Sitting On Top Of The World', 'Carolina In The Morning', 'Rock-a-Bye Your Baby With A Dixie Melody' and 'April Showers'.

The trio's first Parlophone album under Geoff's direction, *Three Kings and an Ace* (PMC 1060) was released in 1958. Complete with the Rita Williams Singers and pianist Ralph Dollimore, it showcases the group's versatility on long standing show tunes such as 'Swinging On A Star', 'Buttons And Bows', 'Surrey With The Fringe On Top' and

'Hallelujah!' The album's opening track, 'That's Entertainment' was a shining example of Geoff's masterful skill and as the sleeve notes point out, illustrates precisely why he was considered one of the greatest British arrangers of all time. Capitalising on its success, EMI repeated the formula two years later with *Kings of Song* (Encore 106) featuring such standards as 'Lullaby Of Broadway', 'Manhattan', 'I'm Sitting On Top Of The World', as well as their big hit 'White Sport Coat' and six of the tracks from the first album.

In 1957 and 1958 Blackpool-born Joan Savage recorded eight songs with Geoff and his orchestra that are still important to collectors. 'Shake Me, I Rattle', backed with 'Lula Rock-a-Hula' (DB 4039) being the most sought-after), then 'Love Letters In The Sand' (DB 3968), 'Bamboozled' (DB 3929) and 'Hello Happiness, Goodbye Blues' (DB 4159).

Dennis Lotis, born in Johannesburg, South Africa, moved to Britain in the 1950s and soon took up with the Ted Heath Orchestra singing alongside Lita Roza and Dickie Valentine. In 1958 he recorded with Geoff and his orchestra, 'Gretna Green', released by Columbia (DB 4090) and once more in 1960, singing 'I Wish It Were You' and 'Love Me A Little', also on Columbia (DB 4432).

Courtesy Brian Foskett

Born Patricia Sibley in 1923, 'Anne Shelton' came to prominence as the Forces sweetheart during World War II. She recorded with Geoff and his orchestra during the 1950s.

Authors collection

Blackpool-born Joan Savage recorded with Geoff and his Orchestra during the 1950's.

Author's collection

South African-born singer Dennis Lotis recorded titles with Geoff and his orchestra, 1958-1960.

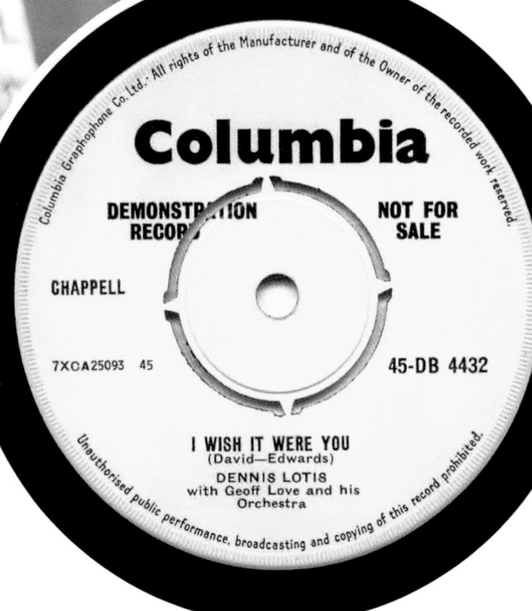

HD 224215

CERTIFIED COPY of an ENTRY OF DEATH
Pursuant to the Births and Deaths Registration Act 1953

Registration District TODMORDEN

1949 . **Death in the Sub-district of** Todmorden **in the** County of York (WR)

Columns: -	1	2	3	4	5	6	7	8	9
No.	When and where died	Name and surname	Sex	Age	Occupation	Cause of death	Signature, description, and residence of informant	When registered	Signature of registrar
468	Twenty Third June 1949 5 SunVale Avenue Walsden Todmorden U.D	Jane MAYCOCK	Female	79 years	widow of Johnson Ambler MAYCOCK Actor	I (a) Myocardial failure (b) Hyperpiesis (c) Arterio Sclerosis	G. Kerr Daughter (*) Present at the death 7. Clarence Street Openshaw Manchester	Twenty fourth June 1949	J. Raby Registrar.

(*) Gladys – 2nd born.

Certified to be a true copy of an entry in a register in my custody.

Dorothy M Baldwin Deputy Superintendent Registrar

31st May 2012 Date

WARNING: A CERTIFICATE IS NOT EVIDENCE OF IDENTITY.

Death certificate of Geoff's grandmother.

Author's collection

'Gimme the moonlight'...... Frankie Vaughan recorded numerous singles with Geoff over the years.

Courtesy of Parlophone Records Limited

First Published 1958.

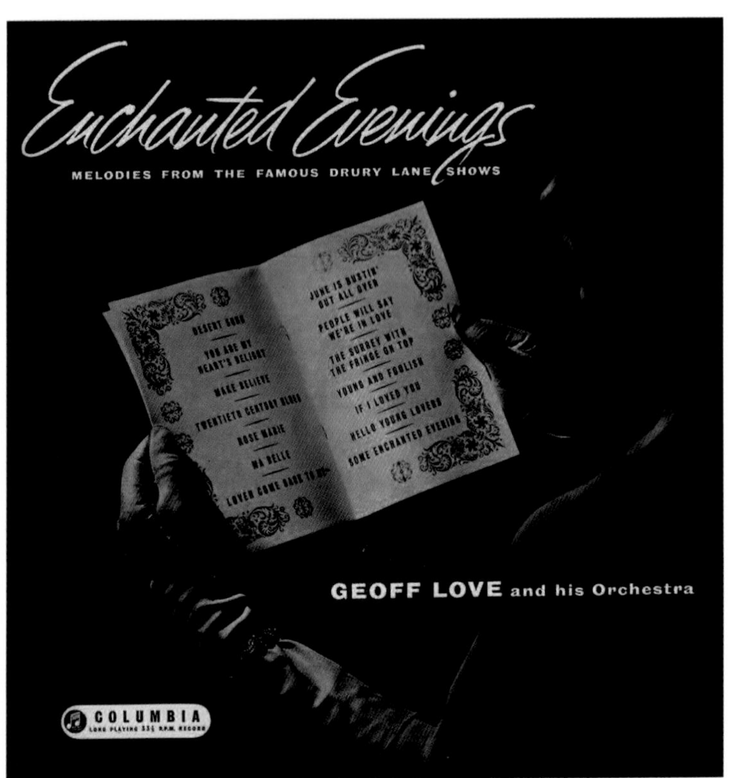

Courtesy of Parlophone Records Limited

First Published 1957.

Courtesy of Parlophone Records Limited

First Published 1957.

Courtesy of Parlophone Records Limited

First Published 1958.

Courtesy Norman Newell

Relatively unknown schoolboy Laurie London became an overnight sensation, after recording with Geoff and his orchestra in November, 1957.

Capitol RECORDS
A Souvenir
from
Miss SHOWBUSINESS
OF YOUR VISIT TO THE
GALA PREMIÈRE OF
"THE JUDY GARLAND SHOW"
HELD AT THE DOMINION THEATRE, LONDON, OCTOBER 16th, 1957
WITH THE COMPLIMENTS OF CAPITOL RECORDS
CAPITOL ARTISTES mean CAPITAL ENTERTAINMENT

Courtesy Norman Newell - photo Richi Howell

Judy Garland hits a high note rehearsing at Abbey Road studios with Geoff and producer Norman Newell, 11th October, 1957.

Courtesy Norman Newell - photo Richi Howell

Geoff and Judy make a final check before Norman directs the recording procedure.

Thing's Getting You Down?
then
Smile, Smile, Smile
with **Mrs. Mills and Geoff**

Publicity card

Courtesy Norman Newell

Once dubbed the 'most popular entertainers of American troops in England', the spiritual – R&B – singing, Deep River Boys, recorded a number of titles with Geoff and his orchestra during the 1950s.

Author's collection

MGM star Howard Keel recorded with Geoff during the 1950s.

First Published 1959.

Courtesy of Parlophone Records Limited

In 1953, Yorkshire-born Jean Carson recorded a single with Geoff and his orchestra for Philips, 'Barrels and Barrels of Roses' / 'A Shoulder to Weep On' (PB.107). She had just become an over-night star in a London stage musical and, on changing her name to Jeannie, went on to fame and fortune in the United States. She became a national institution on television and even has a star on the Hollywood Walk of Fame. Visiting Britain in 1958 she was reunited with Geoff and his orchestra, recording a selection of Scottish songs that HMV released as a picture-sleeve 45EP (7EG8412): 'An Eriskay Love Lilt', 'The Arran Homing Song', 'Ye Banks And Braes' and 'In The Gloaming'. She followed this with a single, 'Ask Me A Question', (POP515).

In the summer of 1958 Latin-American specialist Perez Prado had a runaway success with his cha-cha-cha number, 'Patricia', and Geoff's version, recorded to perfection with his Latin American Rhythm (Columbia DB 4169) became equally so. During the same year, he recorded the first of many long playing albums with Russ Conway for Columbia called *Pack Up Your Troubles* (33SX1120). Typical of its 20 happy-go-lucky melodies were 'For Me And My Gal', 'Pack Up Your Troubles', 'Nellie Dean', 'If You Knew Susie' and 'Underneath The Arches'.

Troubles had no trouble in becoming a best seller and having additional juke box appeal, soon found itself re-issued as a 45EP retitled *Join In With Russ*. Geoff and the popular pianist became inseparable friends, their natural rapport so much in evidence on more Columbia LPs such as *Piano Requests*, *Family Favourites*, *Songs To Sing In Your Bath*, *Russ Hour*, *Enjoy Yourself*, *Time To Play* and *Happy Days*.

During 1959 they had no fewer than five 'top ten' hits totalling more than 70 weeks in the charts, a feat equalled only in that decade by Irish pop star Ruby Murray (1955). That same year, as if paying tribute to his father, Geoff put a small band together that he called *The Rag Pickers* and with Russ at the piano, recorded a few numbers for Columbia that were once the basis of Kidd Love's vaudeville sand dance routine; 'Temptation Rag', 'Twelfth Street Rag', 'That's a Plenty' and the classic 'Russian Rag' (SEG 7886).

Russ Conway

"When I was working for music publisher Chappells in late 1955 I received a call from Lita Roza, top vocalist with the Ted Heath Band who had by then gone solo and she asked me to come to rehearsal rooms just around the corner to help with a routine she was planning for a particular song."

"I toddled off up one flight of stairs to the room where Lita was working and it was then I met, for the first time, Geoff Love who was to become my friend and musical arranger for many years to come. Although at the time I had no idea as to how this relationship would evolve, yet alone me becoming a recording artist."

"I played for Lita in the way she had anticipated, and Geoff worked out the arrangement which suited her. I think my memory is correct when I say that the song was one of many entered for a competition, and Lita was the singer chosen to project the songs for a panel to judge later."

"After that I kept bumping into Geoff, here and there, BBC Broadcasting Studios etc, sometimes as rehearsal pianist for other singers. It was as rehearsal pianist for recording manager Norman Newell that I eventually came to work regularly with Geoff Love."

"By this time I had already discovered his lovely sense of humour and friendly helpful attitude to everyone he worked with. I was glad to know him and when, early in 1957, while acting as Norman's rehearsal pianist, it was decided to turn me into Russ Conway. It was Geoff I relied on totally to help me through my first recording, which 1 made in that year. I was nervous and almost frightened, but he was able to put me so much at ease that I got through that session without a nervous breakdown."

"Recordings I made came thick and fast after EMI Records gave me a ten-year contract and always there was Geoff at the side of the piano, giggling along with the other musicians, keeping everyone at ease and conducting the arrangement with his superb expertise. His body movements, when conducting, also dictated the tempo and it was well nigh impossible to play away from that tempo. He was a brilliant musician and arranger and became so much in demand as the years passed with Stars like Judy Garland, Mel Tormé, Shirley Bassey, Vera Lynn and many many more. But he was always available for me when I needed him."

"I recall the time when I was making my very own first television series for BBC Television, and Jimmy Gilbert was the producer. It had become known that at one time in my life I had learned to play the tuba, so since Geoff was a trombonist himself, it was decided that we do a duet on screen and it wasn't until years later that Geoff confessed to me that he was just as, if not more nervous than I was at the prospect. But, it worked and we enjoyed the fun of it all."

"I really can't think how I would have gone through my career without Geoff Love. A man loved and admired by fellow musicians and millions of listeners to his recordings, both as Geoff Love and also as *Manuel and his Music of the Mountains*. I recently heard his recording of *Moon River* and recalled one session we were doing where I was on the piano with the orchestra during a recording of singer Danny Williams. Danny is also black, as Geoff was, and at one stage in the arrangement the music went from a white note key to a black note key, but I misread my part and went to the next white note key. Whereupon Geoff stopped the orchestra, and turning to me, said, "I've heard of a colour bar, but this is too much". There was humorous uproar from the players, including Danny Williams, but this was the sense of humour which got Geoff and hundreds of others through some very nervous moments during recording."

"I never heard a word spoken against him, and neither did I ever hear himself speak badly of another. He loved life and life loved him. How else could it have possibly been with a name life Geoff LOVE. I miss him still, and also his lovely happy wife Joy, who followed Geoff about a year after his death. Somewhere he will be conducting a heavenly orchestra I think, making sounds which can only bring Joy and Love."

* * * * *

Columbia released Geoff's first big band album, *Heat Wave*, towards the end of 1959. With a big brass section and plenty of percussion it was full of excitement, latin rhythm and mood swings on the likes of 'Old Black Magic', 'Brazil', 'Tangerine', 'Temptation' and, of course, 'Heat Wave'. It was soon spinning on countless Dansettes and Grundigs up and down the country for, as the album's sleeve notes explained, the entire band had captured Geoff's arrangements perfectly when recording them on one of the hottest days of the year's very own heatwave. Sales were outstanding, prompting a later reissue on Columbia's *Encore* label (ENC 187) and later, a 45EP (ESG 7817) using a photo-sleeve of the original LP cover.

Courtesy Russ Conway

A moment of relaxation for Russ Conway, Geoff, his musical director and the Beverley Sisters during rehearsal for the *Russ Conway Show* shown on BBC TV, Friday, 18 March, 1960.

TODMORDEN PRESS BALL COMMITTEE.

ANNUAL PRESS BALL

VERBENA ESPANOLA

(Spanish Night Festival)

TODMORDEN TOWN HALL

September 23rd. Dancing 8 p.m. to 2 a.m.

Lois Sager and her Hammond Organ.

Belvedere Dance Orchestra.

Tony Hall Quartet.

Cabaret.

Personal Appearance of GEOFF. LOVE

(Musical Director E.M.I. Records, Radio Luxembourg and Television).

M.C.s: CLIFFORD POTTS and DOROTHY WILSON.

TICKETS (limited to 350): 12/6.

OVER £300 IN PRIZES. 1960

The Rocking Horse Cowboy * Russ Conway **mono**

First Published 1959

Courtesy of Parlophone Records Limited

Courtesy Bill Francis – Flair Photos

EMI Party: Geoff with left to right: Pete Murray, Jimmy Henney, Tony Osborne, Ray Anthony, Syd Green, David Jacobs, Derek Chinnery and Josephine Douglas.

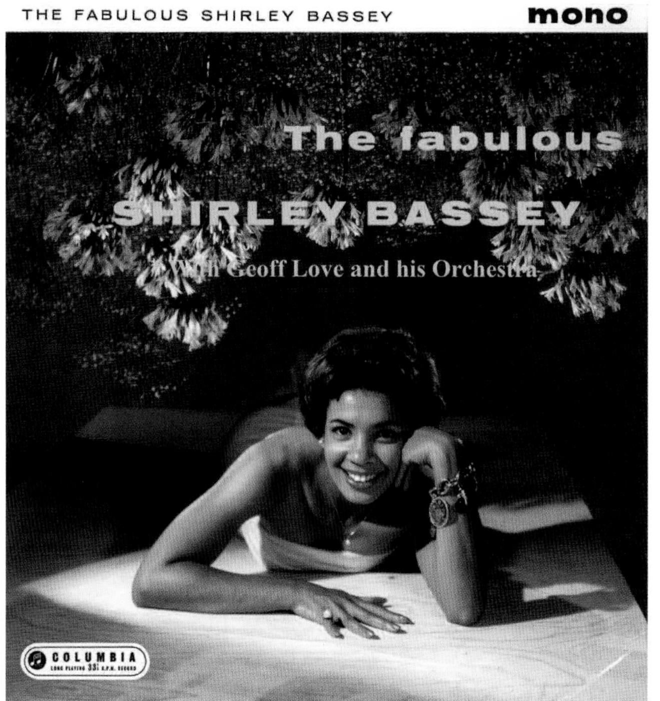

First Published 1959.

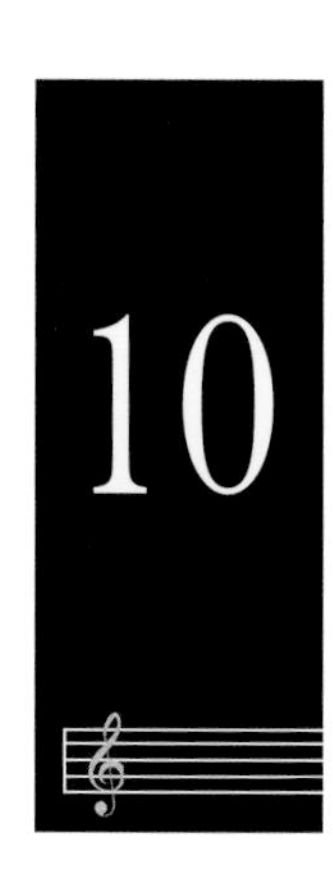

In 1959 Columbia recorded the first of three albums Geoff made with Shirley Bassey who at the time was herself on the brink of stardom. Like Geoff, she had earlier cut some sides for the Philips label but once contracted to EMI producer Norman Newell decided to showcase her magic with a programme of marvellous standards arranged and conducted by Geoff with his orchestra. Entitled *The Fabulous Shirley Bassey* most of the songs were show tunes, including 'A Foggy Day In London Town', 'S'Wonderful', 'Easy To Love', 'I'll Remember April' and 'The Party's Over'. Immediately the recording was completed, and sensing its huge potential, Geoff, with a beaming smile, clapped his hands and said "When do we begin another?" His judgment was spot on, for the album was issued worldwide, reissued on the budget Music For Pleasure label as *The Wonderful Shirley Bassey* (MFP50043) and subsequently on EMI CD 72343 4 98934 (stereo) using the original LP title.

Early in 1961, following Shirley's successful appearance in New York, they teamed up again at the Abbey Road London studios to record a second album. Using the same format, the standards flowed like champagne, with Cole Porter's 'In The Still Of The Night' setting the perfect scene. Shirley was soaring to the moon on 'I'm Shooting High' and proved the old adage that someone could "sure pick 'em", with perfect takes of ten more, including 'If I Were A Bell', 'So In Love', 'Too Late Now' and 'I'm In The Mood For

Love'. Simply called *Shirley* (Columbia 33SX 1286 and SCX 3352 (Stereo) the album became a second best seller, reissued on EMI Starline (SRS 5001) using the title of the opening track and subsequently on EMI CD 7243 4 73226 with the original LP title.

Their third album, entitled *Shirley Bassey* (Columbia 33SX 1382 and SCX 3352 (stereo) was released later in 1961 with yet another inspired choice of standards all showcasing Geoff's outstanding arrangements. This time the numbers featured the additional backing of the Rita Williams Singers and included 'Angel Eyes', 'Fools Rush In', 'Where Or When', 'A Lovely Way To Spend An Evening' and 'Love Is A Many Splendored Thing'.

Shirley's Top Twenty hits under Geoff's direction started in 1959 with the single 'The Party's Over', selected from the first LP. As soon as the other two were recorded in 1960 she made the hit single 'As Long As He Needs Me' and in 1961 hit the jackpot with five more. Never to be forgotten were 'Climb Every Mountain', 'You'll Never Know', 'Reach For The Stars', 'I'll Get By' and 'Hold Me Tight'. There were others over the next two years, including 'Ave Maria', 'Till' and 'Far Away' (from Lionel Bart's "Blitz").

In 1963 Columbia released a picture-sleeve EP with Shirley in sparkling form on four classic standards, showcasing more of Geoff's outstanding arrangements. Titled *In Other Words*, it was something of a masterpiece, starting with the title song (better known as 'Fly Me To The Moon'). Never in finer voice, she then proceeded with 'Just One Of Those Things', 'It's Magic' and 'The Song Is You'.

EMI's budget label Starline then released two albums containing previously unreleased numbers Shirley recorded under Geoff's direction, all evergreens. 'If You Love Me', 'Moon River' and 'Tonight' (from "West Side Story") were featured on SRS 5032 (stereo). Additionally, 'Count On Me', 'It Might As Well Be Spring' and 'You'll Never Walk Alone' were issued on SRS 5092 (stereo). An assortment of eight tracks selected from all the aforementioned were later released by World Record Club on ST 1011 (stereo).

Pepe Jaramillo (born Chihuahua, Mexico, 1921) had a meteoric rise to fame and fortune after moving from Paris to live in London in the late 1950s. A self-taught pianist, he later studied privately with a director of the Mexican Conservatory of Music and developed an exceptional talent for playing every known type of Latin American rhythm. He became popular on radio and television in Mexico City, was a much sought-after accompanist by visiting artists and singers, though at the time the number of his recordings bore no comparison to what came later.

In London he appeared on a BBC radio programme *Stairway to the Stars* and, after hearing an appeal on television for new artists, sent samples of some of his Mexican recordings to Norman Newell. His reaction was immediately positive, visualising Geoff as the ideal musical director in a partnership that lasted 20 years and brought more than the same number of albums. Initially they were recorded with the *Parlophone* label (1959-1965) thereafter on the *Columbia* "Studio 2 Stereo" series. Almost all were issued in Australia and a number in Japan.

A few examples are:

1959 – *Mexico Tropicale,* Parlophone PMC 1080
1960 – *Mexican Fiesta*, Parlophone PMC 1126
1961 – *Salud Mexico*, Parlophone PMC 1147
1962 – *A Mexican on Broadway*, Parlophone PMC 1183
1963 – *Mexican Pizza*, Parlophone PMC 1203
1966 – *Carnival in Mexico*, Columbia Studio 2 Stereo TWO 147
1967 – *Moonlight in Mexico*, Columbia Studio 2 Stereo TWO 182

Peggy Spencer, the well-known British dance teacher, is reported as saying "You haven't lived if you haven't danced to Pepe Jaramillo". He died in his sleep on April 30, 2001, at his home in Mijas, near Malaga, Spain.

In April, 1961, Geoff became the first person to record commercially Eric Spear's theme from the highly popular ITV series *Coronation Street*. More upbeat than the TV version, the Columbia single (DB 4627) was soon on its way to become a best seller.

INTERVIEW WITH TEDDY JOHNSON AT EMI, LONDON. Wednesday 29th March 2000.

– QUOTE: –

"Pearl and I are so pleased to hear of this biography of Geoff Love. It's long overdue and deserving of one of the most talented and respected musical directors who have ever worked in the British recording and television industries. He excelled in all aspects of life without even trying; a natural musician, a natural entertainer and a natural, warm, kind-hearted human being!

I first met Geoff at a social evening at Norrie Paramor's home although I'd heard him often on broadcasts of Harry Gold's Pieces of Eight and I remember seeing him in the trombone section of Norrie's orchestra on my first EMI recording, "Beloved Be Faithful". Our paths crossed again at a concert recorded for Radio Luxembourg when he made a guest appearance with Harry Gold's band and not long afterwards Pearl and I recorded for Polydor with Geoff as musical director. Later at EMI/Columbia we made several more and count ourselves lucky to have been given Geoff as our musical director by producer Norman Newell.

Geoff had become a man of enormous talent, directing his marvellous orchestra on recordings for many of the world's top stars. Joy, his wife and only girlfriend, was such a charming and thoughtful lady who supported him all the way through life. Often at weekends we relaxed with them, sometimes at the Mayfield Club, at a dinner party or just joined them for a drink at the local pub. We miss them both dearly and will treasure those memories for the rest of our lives".

* * * * * *

In October, 1960, Geoff assembled his orchestra and the Rita Williams Singers to record an album at Abbey Road with the Peters Sisters. Hailing from California, the trio's first big success was at New York's Cotton Club, singing with Duke Ellington and his Orchestra. After the war they toured the United States and Canada and later, Europe and in 1959 Norman Newell heard them during a season at the London Palladium. He tied them to a contract the following year when he went to hear them at a summer season show at Blackpool. The album, issued in 1961 on Columbia 33SCX 1288, was a polished, swinging, happy-go-lucky affair, full of standards, proved quite popular and was reissued some years later. No wonder, either, with hit numbers such as 'T'aint What You Do' (It's the way that cha do it), 'Sing Baby Sing', 'It's D'lovely', 'The Best Things In Life Are Free' and 'Please Don't Talk Aout Me When I'm Gone', etc. It should be noted that Columbia released a single prior to the album, recorded at the same session (DB 4400) the songs being 'Ragtime' and 'Ac-Cent-Tchu-Ate The Positive'.

* * * * * *

In 1961, some-time jazz pianist, composer and later front-rank music publisher Joe Henderson (tagged "Mr Piano") recorded his début album for Parlophone. Ably accompanied by Geoff's 22-piece orchestra and the Rita Williams Singers, it was packed with 14 nostalgic numbers such as 'Tangerine', 'Nancy' (with the laughing face), 'Long Ago And Far Away', 'Be Careful, It's My Heart' and 'I'll Get By'. Two versions were issued, mono (PMC 1161) and stereo (PCS 3024).

Courtesy Bill Francis – "Flair Photos"

With Johnny Pearson, Shirley Bassey, Abbey Road studios, Sept., 1959.

Courtesy Norman Newell – photo by Ron Chapman

'Take thee this rose........' with Shirley Bassey, 1959, at Abbey Road studios.

Geoff Love collection – Photo by Ron Chapman

With good friends and recording stars Pearl Carr and Teddy Johnson.

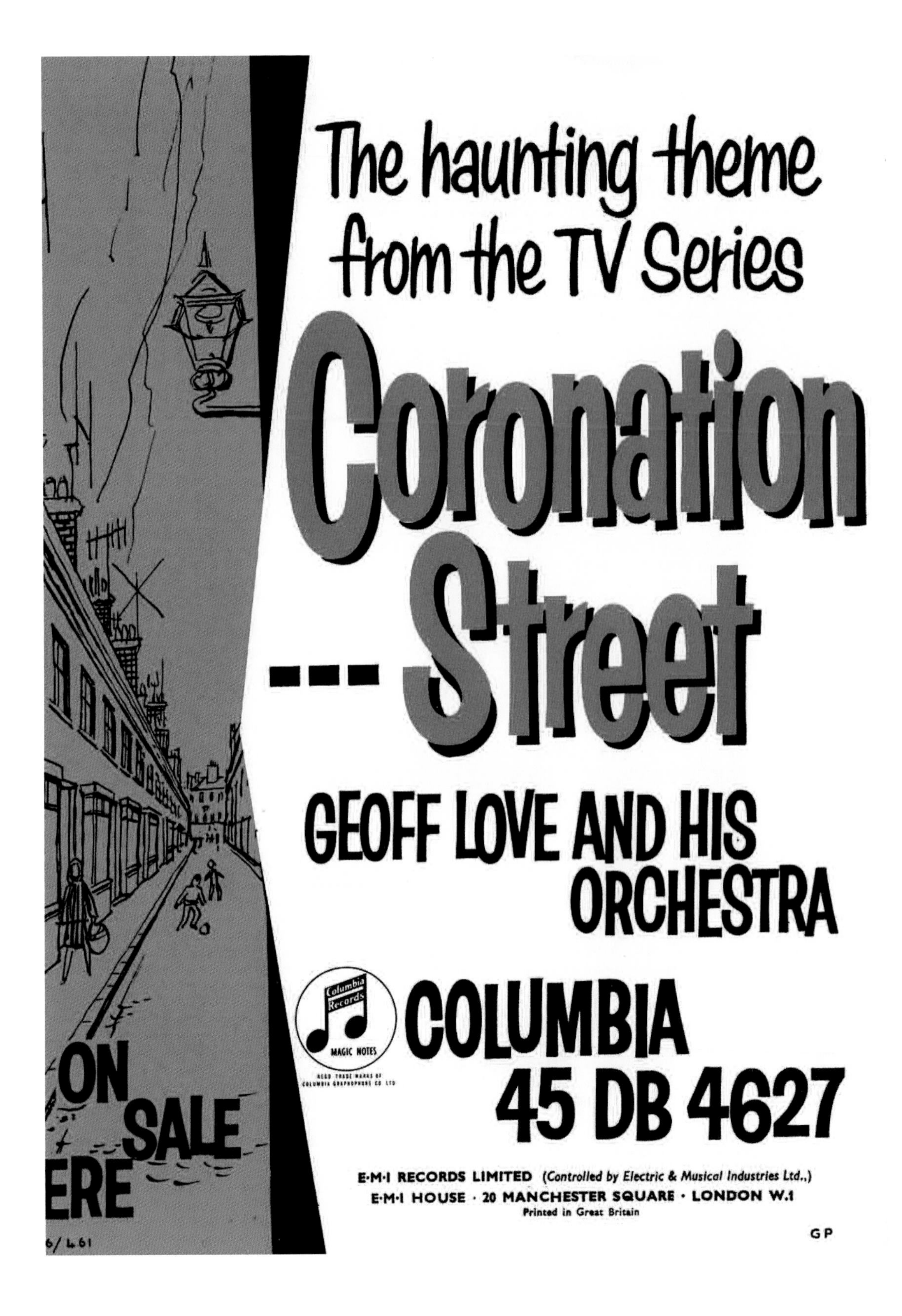
The haunting theme
from the TV Series
Coronation
--- Street
GEOFF LOVE AND HIS
ORCHESTRA
Columbia Records
MAGIC NOTES
COLUMBIA
45 DB 4627
ON
SALE
E·M·I RECORDS LIMITED (Controlled by Electric & Musical Industries Ltd.,)
E·M·I HOUSE · 20 MANCHESTER SQUARE · LONDON W.1
Printed in Great Britain
GP

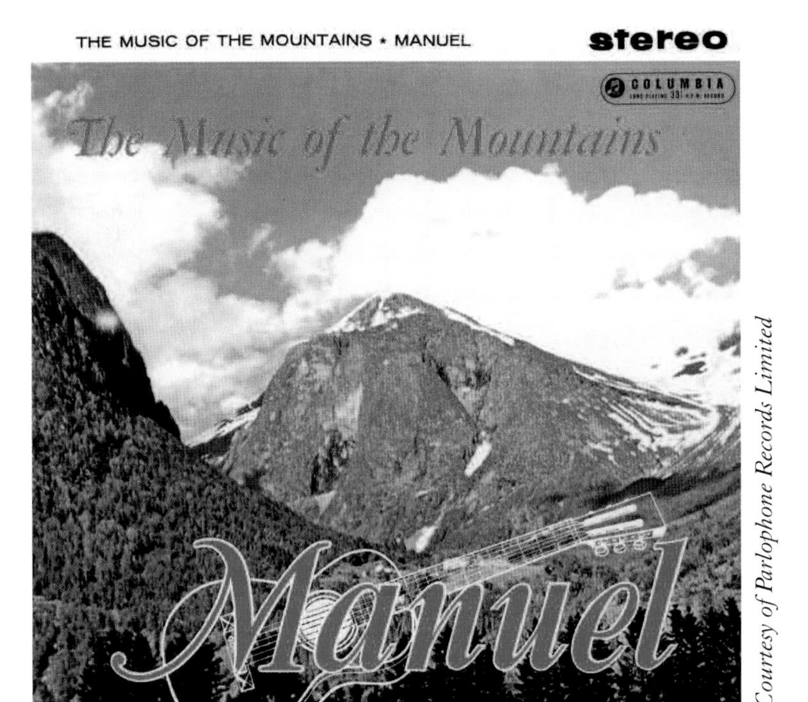

First Published 1960.

Courtesy of Parlophone Records Limited

Producer Norman Newell provided the initial spark for what became the best-selling albums of *Manuel And His Music Of The Mountains*. As the 1959 summer approached, he asked Geoff to view a forthcoming Greek movie called *Manolis* and create a big glamorous sound based on lush strings, suggesting lots of additional acoustic guitars and then compose a film score for the soundtrack from the already approved basic theme by Sansom-Theadorakis. At the end of August, when issued as a single by *Manuel and his Music of the Mountains*, sales of 'The Honeymoon Song' (Columbia DB4323) were so spectacular that Love and Newell immediately formed a separate business partnership to produce more of the same. Without mentioning Geoff or his orchestra, all the initial album covers used panoramic mountain views and were presented as *Manuel and his Music of the Mountains*. They made more than two dozen of them which became popular worldwide, especially so in South America where they were produced at the Mexico City plant of *Capitol Records*. By 1974 sales had exceeded three million and some have since been made available on compact disc. In February 1976 a *Manuel* single made the hit parade with 'Rodrigo's Guitar Concerto de Aranjuez', reached No. 3 and stayed in the charts for 10 weeks. With such a long-winded title who would have predicted this, yet more followed, especially the music score 'Somewhere My Love' from the film *Doctor Zhivago* and the title theme from Jules Dassin's earlier *Never On Sunday*.

In 1979, Geoff recorded the first digital album produced at Abbey Road. Called *Super Natural* and released in the Manuel and his Music of the Mountains series (Studio Two stereo TWO D2001) the album's unique recording technique was fully explained on the LP sleeve. Using two special stereo digital recorders designed and built by EMI's central research laboratories at Hayes, Middlesex, the orchestra musicians became astounded when listening to the pure quality of the recording's playback. The process was repeated for the following two Manuel recordings, namely *Fiesta* (TWO D2002) and *Fantasy* (TWO D2004) issued in 1980 and 1981, respectively.

In September 1955, Geoff appeared with an orchestra on Independent Television's first Saturday transmission, after which ABC Television signed him to a contract and made him musical director. Success came immediately with a Sunday night special called *Sentimental Journey* and then he was featured in a 54 week series called *On The Town* which originally had been scheduled for only seven programmes. During 1960/61 he was seen regularly directing the orchestra on the *Russ Conway Show*, the best rated on TV in January, 1961, and on the *Dickie Valentine Show* during 1966. He also composed the theme music for what became two of the highest-rated shows on television - *Bless This House* and *This Is Your Life*, of which he was the subject himself in 1975.

The programme was filmed by Thames Television during the morning and afternoon of New Year's Eve, 1974, and shown on January 8. It began with presenter Eamonn Andrews marching the Todmorden Old Brass Band along the avenue leading to Geoff's Enfield home at 26, Queen Anne's Place. He was appropriately attired, complete with peaked cap, as being the band's official conductor. Gathering everyone around the front porch, he greeted the amazed bandleader with the immortal words, "Geoffrey Love – this is your loyf"!

One band member, Philip Kerr, remembers it all in vivid, amazing detail.

Philip Kerr

"The initial approach came from Thames Television in January, 1974, asking if the band would be available to play on 31 December in London for no fee, but all expenses paid. The engagement details were not divulged at that time. We travelled down by coach and had some breakfast, which it turned out, had to sustain us until much later in the day. We met with Eamonn Andrews and discovered that we were to march up to Geoff's front door playing.

However, all was not as well as it seemed as an official from the Musicians Union demanded that only musicians in the Union would be allowed to play. Then Thames Television would only agree to pay to enrol 12 of us, the other 14 would have to (supposedly) mime. And so it went on. Eamonn was unable to march in time with the band so had one of his production team to march out of camera shot so that he could watch and copy him. When Geoff saw us at his front door, genuinely astonished, his wonderful smiling face greeted us with the immortal lines "Tod Band! Where's the pies and peas?": it being a reference to post-concert parties at the Queen or White Hart hotels, (when pie and peas were inevitably served) at the conclusion of charity concerts at the Tod Town Hall at which Geoff had conducted the band.

On the journey home later that night, one of the band members, Bill Howard, produced a script of the show that he'd "opportuned", which revealed that once Eamonn had entered Geoff's home they had rehearsed the programme details, with specific lines to answer in response to Eamonn and the guests. Not surprising perhaps, in hindsight, that the recording should be so carefully planned and organised".

The show opened with Geoff and his wife Joy being congratulated by their first-born son Adrian, followed by second son, Nigel, and his wife, Diana, Geoff's mother, Frances and his sister, Connie. Max Bygraves, Diana Coupland, Beryl Reid and Norrie Paramour were unswerving with compliments, not just about Geoff's ability as a musician and skill as a musical director, but how much respect they had for him as a warm-hearted, caring person and friend. There were also filmed tributes from Frankie Vaughan, Frank Ifield and Mrs Mills, none of whom could be present owing to prior commitments.

More praise came from his great friend and producer Norman Newell and from his first employer, Edwin Shawforth, of Todmorden. Freddy Platt, whose band he had joined when only 16, came from Rochdale, expressing happy memories and compliments as did jazz bandleader Harry Gold who, with his Pieces of Eight, brought the show to a close with Geoff joining in and singing an up-beat 'Shine', once one of his very own feature spots with the band, almost 30 years before.

* * * * * *

The popularity of this single led to the pressing of more than 3 million albums worldwide and subsequently to demands for CD releases.

Geoff Love collection

Manchester, 1963, to record songs with the Oldham Youth Choir for the BBC play 'Yours for a Song'.

WINTER GARDENS BOURNEMOUTH

EXTER ROAD, BOURNEMOUTH BH2 5AP

Entertainments Manager for Bournemouth Corporation : SAMUEL J. BELL

Box Office Tel. 26446

8.0 – SUNDAY, 20th MAY, 1973 – 8.0

HAROLD LANDEY

FOR MELTON PRODUCTIONS LTD.

PRESENTS

GEOFF LOVE

AND HIS

40-PIECE CONCERT ORCHESTRA

THE PROGRAMME WILL INCLUDE ADAPTATIONS FROM HIS BEST SELLING ALBUMS

"MANUEL AND THE MUSIC OF THE MOUNTAINS"

Prices : £1.60, £1.30, £1.10, 80p

Box Office open each day from 10 a.m. to 5 p.m. (10 a.m. - 8.30 p.m. on concert dates)
Sundays 2 p.m to 8.30 p.m. concert dates only
Seats also bookable at Information Bureau, Boscombe Arcade.

Printed by Electric (Modern) Printing Co. Ltd., Manchester

HAROLD LANDEY

for Melton Productions Ltd.

PRESENTS

geoff love

and his 40-piece concert orchestra

PROGRAMME

The programme will include adaptations from Geoff Love's best-selling albums **'MANUEL AND THE MUSIC OF THE MOUNTAINS'**

SIGNATURE TUNE—LOVE WALKED IN

1. Malagena
2. The Godfather
3. Diamonds Are Forever
4. The Magnificent Seven
5. Moon River
6. Hora Staccato
7. If I Were a Rich Man
8. Autumn Leaves
9. Jealousy
10. Peanut Vendor
11. Big Country

INTERVAL

---

1. Mexican Hat Dance
2. Raindrops Keep Falling On My Head
3. Match of the Day
4. If
5. High Noon
6. Somewhere My Love
7. Sound of Music
8. A Banda
9. Cabaret
10. Judy Garland Medley

The following themes may also be included :

1. Abduls Theme
2. You Made Me Love You
3. The Great Escape March
4. La Bamba
5. La Golondrina

Geoff Love collection

Thames TV studios, London, 31st December, 1974. Left to right: Geoff's son Nigel and wife Diana, sister Cornelia, son Adrian, Geoff's mother Frances, his wife Joy, Max Bygraves, Diana Coupland, Norrie Paramor, Beryl Reid, Norman Newell, Edwin Shawforth.

Courtesy EMI Archives

Geoff recorded four albums and a movie score with international star Connie Francis during the 1960s.

The entertainer with whom Geoff was most closely associated was Max Bygraves. After first consulting with the show's star, Thames TV signed Geoff as musical director for the 1968 series *Max* and as well as arranging and conducting all the show's songs the pair were sometimes seen in on-screen repartee. It became the best-rated show on television during its five-month run and in the follow-up series, *Singalonga-Max* (1973 and 1978) and *Lingalonga-Max* (1979), Geoff was always seen at some point in each show as a comic foil to Max's crafty one-liners. They often appeared together at the *London Palladium*, became good friends on and off screen with the star always prepared to say how wise he had been to choose Geoff as musical director for his inaugural TV series.

Max Bygraves

"For the obituary I wrote in the Guardian on Geoff Love - July 10th, 1991 - the heading was 'Love - a many splendoured man'. I tried to put into words the deep affection and respect that I had - and still have - for the lovely Geoff. We first met in the early 1950s. In those days, Geoff was an arranger and I was recording for the HMV label. In November, 1955, I was to record a song entitled 'Meet me on the corner', a successful Top Ten entry.

We actually named a show after the title which had a long run at the London Hippodrome. The record was a hit because of Geoff's fine arrangement. We met casually over the years. Then in 1968, Thames TV asked me to appear in a series called simply 'Max'. I was given my choice of orchestras and plumped immediately for Geoff. So started a partnership on TV that lasted over 15 years."

"Geoff always had trouble rolling his Rs. For our backchat, the writers, unknown to Geoff would write in lines full of Rs, like: 'The Rolls-Royce is round on the ramp'. When Geoff delivered the line it came out: 'The Wolls-Woyce is wound on the wamp!' Sometimes, to get an extra laugh. I'd say "Geoff. would you mind repeating that?"

"Geoff also recorded as *Manuel and his Music of the Mountains*. The musicians he worked with, the cream of British jazz and concert players, soon discovered his knowledge and their respect for him made him the pop scene's most accepted musical director. He provided orchestral backings for Shirley Bassey. Russ Conway and many more top recording stars. In between, he gave his time to the Stars Organisation for Spastics. His happiest days were spent in Spain where he was water-skiing up to a short time before his death."

"When work permitted, he and his lovely wife Joy would go off in his Jaguar to snatch a few days in Sitges, south of Barcelona. He'd return and show off his suntan. The grandson of a Cherokee Indian, it was difficult to see, but he assured us that it was there. Even Joy, a born and bred English lady, would shake her head in disbelief."

"On one of his last trips to Spain he was mugged. It happened just outside Lyons in France. He was flagged down by a conman in another car. When Geoff slowed down, the man pointed to the back wheel and Geoff stopped and got out to see what was wrong. An accomplice jumped into the driving seat and was away with the Jaguar, plus all Geoff's belongings, passport and money and so on. Geoff told me all this over the phone when he got back. "I don't suppose you'll feel like going to Spain again, will you Geoff?" I asked. "Oh yes", he replied. "I don't feel the same without a suntan!""

"Love was his name and love was his nature. To me he seemed indestructible and his death came as a great shock."

* * * * * *

Far from retreating into television though, Geoff's work at EMI's recording studios increased and for a time he became the most recorded artist in the country. What's more, he could always rely on some of London's best session musicians to make up the best possible orchestra. Former Ted Heath trombonist Don Lusher was one of them,

Todmordian Ken Goldie, former trombone player with Vic Lewis and Ted Heath, was another while double bassist Arthur Watts became an ever-present in the rhythm section. Almost always in the string section was Norman Barker, a highly respected London session musician who had once been the leader of the Todmorden semi-pro band who had given Geoff his first gigs as a young teenager back in the 1930s.

Don Lusher

"I worked for Geoff for many years, mainly in the studios and am certain that all the musicians in his various orchestras respected his musicianship and arranging skills as much as I did. We all enjoyed working for him. He and his wife were wonderful people and it was sad when Geoff and then Joy passed away. He had lots of friends in showbusiness and I'm sure that, like myself, they all miss him".

* * * * * *

Recording studios held little attraction for some top stars. Without a live audience and under the closest scrutiny they saw them as the cold light of day where nothing was left to chance and where temperament mattered as much as anything. So genuine was the warmth of Geoff's personality that, no matter what the occasion or how famous the star, he had natural ability to put everyone present completely at ease. Calling for a fourth or fifth "take" (still another recording of the tune just played) was not his style. Leading artists with whom he recorded included Judy Garland, Marlene Dietrich, Connie Francis, Joni James, Vera Lynn, Shirley Bassey, Eartha Kitt, Gracie Fields, Mel Tormé, Paul Robeson, Johnny Mathis, Howard Keel, Russ Conway, the King Brothers, Pearl Carr and Teddy Johnson, Frankie Vaughan, Alma Cogan, Marion Ryan, the Beverley Sisters, Anne Shelton, Tommy Steele, Danny La Rue, Danny Williams, Norman Wisdom, Ken Dodd, Des O'Connor, Clinton Ford and Mrs Mills, many of whom had the greatest affection for him.

The three Beverley Sisters were often in the Top Twenty during the 50s and 60s. Known to sing in close harmony, sometimes with a risque element, they had their own TV series and even became popular in the United States. They were signed to Columbia and recorded some singles with Geoff and his orchestra, including 'The Skye Boat Song' / 'Green Fields' (DB 4444) and 'I Thought Of You Last Night' / 'The Whole Year Around' (DB 4523).

He recorded countless albums with the ever-smiling/laughing Mrs (Gladys) Mills whose vamping, honky-tonk piano style was a perfect combination with Geoff's happy-go-lucky personality. She was born in 1918 at Bletchley in Buckinghamshire and moved with her parents to Loughton, in Essex, when she was about 12. She had begun piano lessons when only three and won a talent contest when she was 14. After leaving school she became a typist, working in a City office though quite often, at weekends, played for dinner dances with her small band, the Astorians. In 1961, she was spotted at one of them by an agent who recommended her to BBC Television resulting in a sing-along spot playing piano in the Billy Cotton Band Show. Norman Newell soon realised her potential, recording her with Geoff for Parlophone, calling the album *Mrs Mills Medley*. It was released in December of that year and very quickly entered the charts. Likewise, many more, including *Mrs Mills Plays The Roaring Twenties* (PCS 3030), *Mrs Mills' Party* (PMC 1264), *Music For Anytime* (PCS 3070), '*Come To My Party*' (PMC 7010), *Summer Party* (PCS 7046), '*Back To The Roaring Twenties*' (PCS 7080) and '*Glad With Love*' (MFP 50220), with both participants radiating an irresistible 'Come-on-and-join-us' atmosphere.

She became a household name on the BBC and had an exceptionally tricky technique to her "stride playing", a style that came to prominence through the work of pianists like James P. Johnson, Thomas "Fats" Waller, Willie "The Lion" Smith and Charles "Luckey" Roberts and perpetuated later by musicians like Dick Hyman, Dick Wellstood and Ralph Sutton. Her recordings were made under Norman Newell's watchful eye and Geoff's musical direction at London's Abbey Road Studios. Her Steinway upright piano was specially adapted, the hammers being lightly coated with a metallic substance to give it the honky-tonk sound. It has been preserved and holds pride of place within the very studio where her recordings took place. Her life was cut short at the age of 60 when, weighing 16 stone, she died in a Buckingham nursing home on Saturday, 25 February, 1978.

* * * * * *

Courtesy Pearson Television

Max Bygraves signed Geoff as musical director for four of his hit TV series. (1968, 1973, 1978 and 1979)

Author's Collection

Todmorden-born Norman Barker, Lic., TCM (died 12th November, 1987).
In later years, a front-line musician in the Mantovani and ATV orchestras and often in Geoff's studio orchestras

Courtesy EMI Archives

Geoff Love, Norman Newell and Paul Robeson at Abbey Road studios, 1960.

Unquestionably one of the most successful female artists of the 50s and 60s, Connie Francis recorded several albums with Geoff and his orchestra at Abbey Road studios.

Courtesy Norman Newell

Author's collection

60s star Marion Ryan record with Geoff and his orchestra for MGM.

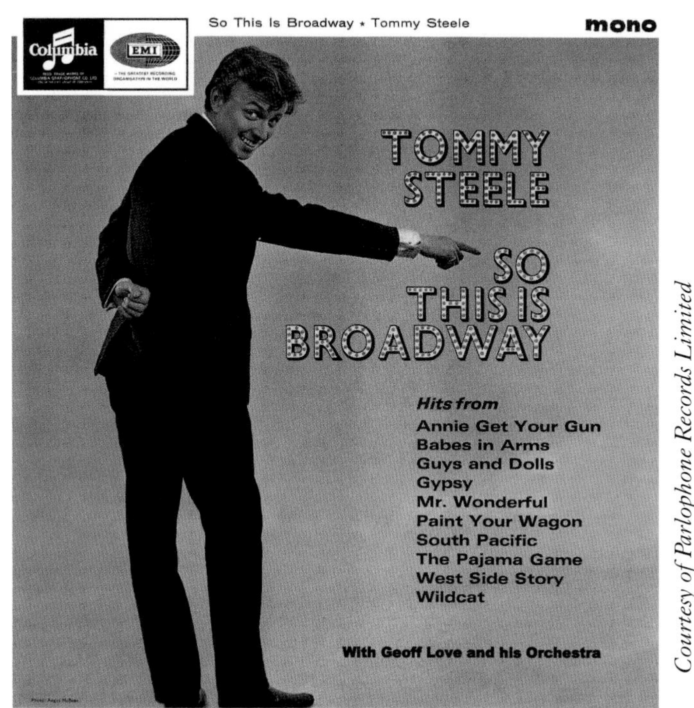

First Published 1964.

Courtesy of Parlophone Records Limited

Released during 1959/60 were four albums Geoff recorded for MGM with top entertainer Connie Francis: *My Thanks to You* (MGM C 782) and later reissued on World Record Club (TTP 618), *Christmas With Connie* (MGM C 797) released simultaneously in the United States as *Christmas In My Heart* (MGM stereo E/SE37902), *Sings Spanish And Latin American Favourites* (MGM C 836) and *Sings Jewish Favourites* (MGM C 845). She was so delighted with Geoff's arrangements and conducting skill that she insisted he orchestrate her songs for her next movie, *Follow The Boys*. Later he provided orchestrations for some of the songs in Tommy Steele's film, *It's All Happening,* in which he also made an appearance. Then, before the effervescent Cockney star took his smash-hit London show *Half A Sixpence* to Broadway he recorded an aptly titled album with Geoff called *So This Is Broadway* (33 SX 1674). Stateside, it was released by Liberty Records under the title *Sixpenny Millionaire* (LST 7566) and reissued in Britain on World Record Club using the original title (TP610 S).

Tommy Steele

"The idea was that, as Half a Sixpence was about to go to America, an album of famous show tunes by me would serve as an introduction to Broadway. So off I went into a world I had never entered before.

Geoff Love was the designated arranger and he presented me with a few ideas for the

style of the score. The first item on his list was 'Something's Coming' from West Side Story. 'You have to trust me on this one.' Geoff smiled, 'It can bite your bum.'
I didn't know what he meant until the day of the session. The orchestra was immense, the arrangement was a magnificent tour de force and I was chucked into the sound booth a wreck. 'I don't know where to pick it up.' I winced. 'The beat keeps changing.' Geoff smiled in his easy going way and held up four fingers. 'That's all it is son,' he beamed. 'Watch the stick and count. There's no trick to it, leave the rest to me and Mister Bernstein'.
How right he was and what a lovely man."

While she was visiting London in 1960, Geoff recorded an album for MGM with leading American singer Joni James who had shot to fame in 1953 with a million-seller single 'Why Don't You Believe Me'. Within a year she was a jukebox idol with a dozen hit-parade singles and later became a prolific MGM recording artist with one of the largest album catalogues of all American popular singers.

Her British début album, *100 Strings and Joni* (MGM C 777), was full of romantic standards such as 'Imagination', 'Body And Soul', 'I Can Dream Can't I', 'It Could Happen To You' and 'It Never Entered My Mind'. Two singles were later issued from the same session, 'There Goes My Heart'/'Funny' (45 MGM 991) and 'You Belong To Me' /'I Need You Now' (45 MGM 1064).

In 1961, a follow-up album was released, *100 Strings and Joni In Hollywood* (MGM C 839), and in 1962 a third, *100 Strings and Joni On Broadway* (MGM C 865).

* * * * * *

Immortalised during the Second World War as the "Forces' Sweetheart", Vera Lynn's romantic and soothing songs brought comfort and hope to the millions who suffered during those bleak years. Almost as famous then as Winston Churchill, she became one of the quintessential British singers and recorded her first album with Geoff and his orchestra for MGM in July, 1960. Called *Sing with Vera* (MGM C 840) and later reissued on its budget label (2353-098) it included some of her wartime favourites, 'Underneath The Arches', 'I'll Be With You In Apple Blossom Time', 'Now Is The Hour', 'We'll Meet Again' and a selection of nostalgic numbers including 'If I Had My Way', 'Cruising Down The River', 'You Made Me Love You', etc.

Its success brought a second album within months, released in the spring of 1961 and called, simply, *Yours* (MGM C 843). Very much in a romantic mood, titles included 'Yours', 'Unforgettable', 'Again', 'You'll Never Know' and 'I'll Be Seeing You'. This time all orchestrations were by Brian Fahey with the Rita Williams Singers once more in harmony with Geoff's impeccable orchestra. It was reissued on MGM's budget label. (2353 085)

Later that same year she recorded a third album with Geoff's orchestra and the Williams Singers. MGM issued this under the title *As Time Goes By* (MGM C 855; MGM CS 6030). The album included the title song and was filled with more romantic melodies such as 'Hello Young Lovers', 'Young At Heart', 'A Lovely Way To Spend An Evening', 'Wee Small Hours Of The Morning' and 'I'll Remember April'. Like its predecessors, the album's success soon brought a reissue under the same title on Music for Pleasure (MFP 1005) and a U.S. pressing (MGM stereo E3889) with the same title. In 1963, forever patriotic and true to her wartime code as the "Forces Sweetheart", she recorded 'Land of Hope and Glory' with Geoff and his orchestra, released by HMV as a single (45 - POP 1111) with 'From the time you say goodbye' as the supporting B side.

Dame Vera Lynn, D.B.E., LL.D., M. Mus.

"Geoff was an outstanding musician who made an immeasurable contribution to the British music scene over a long number of years. His ability and great charm made him a popular figure with everyone he worked with, always cheerful, he helped us all relax. I recorded three albums with him for MGM, one in 1960 and the others the year following."

"He was always my conductor for the Stars Organisation for Spastics Christmas Concerts and usually for all the other stars who regularly took part. Nothing was ever too much trouble for Geoff when it came to writing the show's orchestrations and he is greatly missed by myself and everyone in the S.O.S organisation."

* * * * * *

During 1960 the American actor and bass singer Paul Robeson was on a visit to Britain. His most famous film role had been that of Bosambo in the 1933 African adventure *Sanders of the River,* whose stirring canoe song of the same title had been a hit on both sides of the Atlantic. *HMV* decided to record him in London using Geoff's orchestrations and musical direction plus the Rita Williams singers. Entitled *An Evening With Paul Robeson* (CLP 1415) it contained many classics such as 'I'll Walk Beside You', 'Some Enchanted Evening', 'Land Of My Fathers' and 'Skye Boat Song' and, while having a limited market, sold well enough to reappear later on EMI's *Music For Pleasure* budget label. The outstanding virtuoso, who had even sung and recorded with jazz man Count Basie, died on 23rd January, 1976.

In London during July 1961, Geoff, Tony Osborne and Wally Stott each led their orchestras on an album with top American star Mel Tormé. It was first issued in the U.K. in 1962, called *My Kind of Music* by HMV, in both mono (CLP 1584) and stereo (CSD 1442). It was simultaneously released in the U.S. on Verve V6/8440.

Geoff and his orchestra lit the torch with the opening number, an intense upbeat 'You And The Night And The Music' and intermingling with the other combinations came his orchestrations and backing for 'By Myself', 'The Christmas Song' and 'A Shine On My Shoes'. Geoff had personally chosen the fourth number, a song he had orchestrated earlier and one of his own special favourites. Tormé unhesitatingly agreed and on being asked for his style and tempo, simply said 'Surprise me'. So he did; presented the score in its original form and the song was flawlessly recorded in one take. Producer Norman Newell was so pleased with the outcome that it was soon issued as a single as support to the A side, 'The Christmas Song' (45 MGM 1144).

* * * * * *

In addition to the countless albums Geoff recorded with EMI's top artists Norman Newell and himself seemed to have a second sense for what the public wanted to hear in the easy-listening field and so made scores of others with the concert orchestra using every title imaginable. There were albums of love songs, waltzes, tangos, all manner of movie and TV themes covering westerns, soap operas, thrillers, academy award winners, the James Bond movies, 7 or 8 volumes each of instrumental and banjo favourites, country music, ragtime and Dixie jazz, a Christmas Album and for good measure, an LP of Disney Songs with the Mike Sammes Singers on which Geoff's unmistakeable voice comes through as 'King Louis the Most!' Whereas viewers merely heard the opening few bars of a TV programme's signature tune Geoff arranged and recorded dozens of them in their entirety. It almost seemed as if his workload would never cease for his orchestrating and conducting duties even included an album or two of children's songs and nursery rhymes.

His recordings at Abbey Road continued to accelerate as he and the Sammes troubadours soon teamed up again to record the music and songs from the 1939 MGM muscial fantasy, *The Wizard of Oz*. Released in 1966 in the Music for Pleasure series, (MFP 1118) it showcased Roberta Rex in the role of Dorothy that shot teenager Judy Garland to eternal fame.

Not long after this, Geoff and his orchestra returned to the studio to record the music from Lionel Bart's long-running hit show *Oliver*! This must have been a joyous experience with Jon Pertwee singing the part of Fagin and one-time teenage rock-and-roll idol Jim Dale that of the Artful Dodger. The album became a best seller in the Music for Pleasure series. (MFP 1073).

Geoff's boundless enthusiasm and popularity brought many more successful albums as he formed *the Geoff Love Singers*, *the Geoff Love Banjos, the Geoff Love Mandolins* and in complete contrast, his own *Big Disco Sound*.

* * * * * *

David Jacobs, CBE, DL.

"Behind his easy-going, happy-go-lucky manner, Geoff Love was one of the most brilliant musical directors in the whole of showbusiness, without a wrong word to say about anyone".

"The list of stars with whom he recorded, both British and American, is almost endless. Included were Judy Garland, Marlene Dietrich, Connie Francis, Vera Lynn, Shirley Bassey, Johnny Mathis, Danny Williams and Frankie Vaughan. For a long time it was unknown that it was Geoff and his Orchestra behind Manuel and his Music of the Mountains and his records always played an important part in my radio programme. Years before he'd been on Radio Luxembourg and was in at the opening of the commercial network television with a 54-week series, *On The Town*. He was with Russ Conway and Dickie Valentine in their series and with Max Bygraves on his hit shows. He was ably supported by his charming wife Joy and lived in Enfield with sons Adrian and Nigel".

* * * * * *

Courtesy Norman Newell

Geoff and Tony Osborne shared orchestrating/conducting duties on the 1960 Joni James MGM album, *100 strings and Joni* (MGM c.777).

Courtesy Norman Newell

Joni is clearly impressed with the playback

Courtesy Dame Vera Lynn – photo Ron Chapman

Geoff and producer Norman Newell hear a playback of one of three albums Dame Vera Lynn recorded with Geoff's orchestra during 1960/61.

Author's collection

American headliner Mel Tormé, who recorded with Geoff in 1961.

Courtesy of Parlophone Records Limited

First Published 1975.

Courtesy of Parlophone Records Limited

First Published 1975.

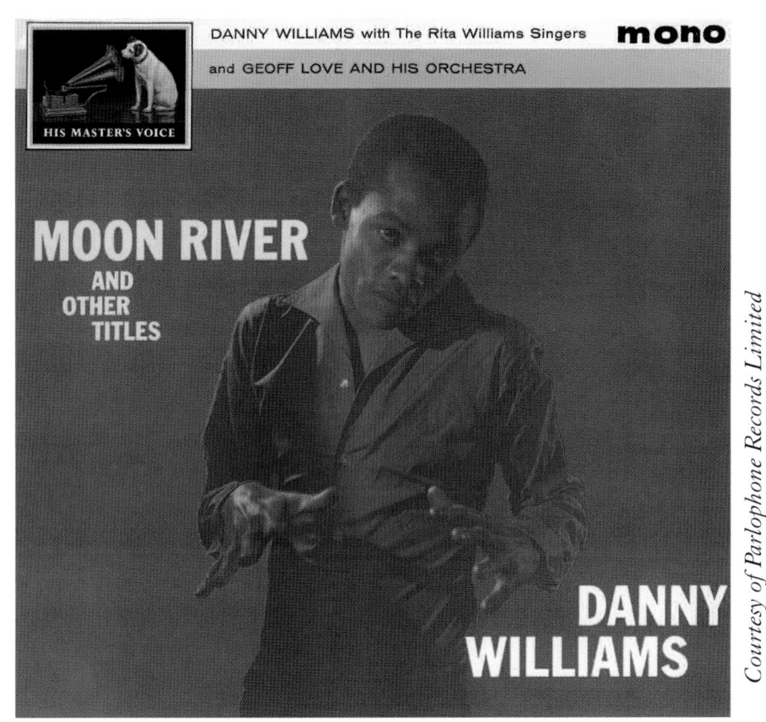

First Published 1961.

Courtesy of Parlophone Records Limited

South African-born singer Danny Williams, who first arrived in Britain during 1959 with a musical revue from his home town Port Elizabeth called *Golden City Dixies,* was soon signed to an HMV contract by Norman Newell. His début album (CLP 1458) in 1961 contained 12 popular songs, some of them standards like 'As Time Goes By', 'Too Young'and 'Danny Boy', eight of them under Geoff's musical direction with the Rita Williams Singers and four numbers accompanied by Tony Osborne and his orchestra.

Subsequently, Geoff and Danny Williams were teamed on dozens of singles that were spun by disc jockeys, the most successful being 'Moon River' (HMV POP 932) which hit the top spot during Nov/Dec, 1961, and stayed in the hit parade for almost five months. The song became the title of his second album (CLP 1521) which included standards like 'My Foolish Heart', 'All Or Nothing At All' and 'I Talk To The Trees'. It became a top seller and once out of print was quickly reissued by World Record Club using the same title (T 669).

Danny Williams

"I first met Geoff Love when I was introduced to him by Norman Newell at EMI House, when it was still sited near Oxford Street."

"I had just taken part in an inadvertent audition at the Metropolitan Theatre, Edgware Road where the touring show *Golden City Dixies* was about to open in which I played a small part."

"Norman Newell had been asked to see the show, in particular to listen to one of the girl singers who had a powerful voice but modelled her style on that of Shirley Bassey. Unfortunately for the girl, Norman was then Shirley's record producer and, for good reason, turned her down. Inexplicably he immediately put his focus on me, although on the day I was not and neither was anyone else there to perform except giving the auditioning girl full vocal and instrumental back-up."

"I was asked to step forward to sing the only song 'Faith Can Move Mountains', a Nat Cole classic that I did in the show. I was told that the producer was very impressed and would I go along down to the auditorium to meet his party. The next thing I remember was being taken to EMI House by Norman and Co. to meet my new musical director, Geoff Love."

"I was only a kid in my early teens, quite nervous, having just stepped off a plane from South Africa, but Geoff immediately put me at ease. He was totally unassuming and gentlemanly for his position, but I have to admit that I had never heard of him at that time."

"Geoff, with his extraordinary expertise for string writing and Norman's aptitude for choosing my recording material, guided my career to the highest point when we recorded and took 'Moon River' from the film *Breakfast at Tiffany's* to number one. Geoff and his orchestra with the Rita Williams Singers backed me on chart follow-ups such as 'Jeannie', 'Wonderful World Of The Young', 'Tears' and others."

"I didn't meet up with Geoff socially as we were from different age groups, though I met his family on a few occasions. His lovely wife Joy was an accomplished pianist and I got on very well with Geoff's eldest son, Adrian, though I only met his youngest son once at the time I visited their home."

"I will always remember Geoff for his gentle nature, how he painstakingly nursed me through all the recordings of which there must have been hundreds. He always had a big, genuine smile and I felt that he treated me either as if I was his son or a kid brother. I do miss him."

* * * * * *

In 1962 Geoff began a long and successful association with Liverpool comedian Ken

Dodd, a man of many talents who two years before had a top ten vocal hit for Decca called 'Love Is Like A Violin'. Columbia signed him to a long-term contract and released his first album *Presenting Ken Dodd* (33SX1479) in 1962 accompanied by Geoff and his orchestra with the Rita Williams Singers. Of their many hit parade singles the most famous was 'Tears' (DB 7659) which hit the top in September 1965 and stayed there for seven weeks. It became a million-seller, brought a gold disc, remained in the charts for five months and was eventually rated the third biggest-selling single of the Sixties, exceeding two million copies.

Sir Ken Dodd

"Working at Columbia with Geoff Love was one of the most enjoyable periods of my career. He was a magnificent musician and a lovely person."

* * * * * *

Glamorous Alma Cogan, who was seldom out of the hit parade during the 1950s, particularly with songs like 'Bell Bottom Blues', 'Little Things Mean A Lot' and 'I Can't Tell A Waltz From A Tango' was originally teamed with musical director Frank Cordell at HMV. Then, in 1960 she signed with Columbia under the guidance of Norman Newell and soon released an album of standards recorded with three different orchestras. Its title song, 'With You In Mind' was performed with Geoff's orchestra together with four other classics, 'But Beautiful', 'Fly Me To The Moon', 'You'll Never Know' and 'The More I See You'. The orchestras of Tony Osborne and Stan Foster provided the others.

The following year came her second, entitled *How About Love?* and no wonder, for with the word "love" appearing in eleven of the songs' titles, all with Tony Osborne's Orchestra, just one number, 'Hello Young Lovers' was recorded with Geoff. Still, she was paired with him on a number of chart entries including her last big hit, 'Cowboy Jimmy Joe', in 1961. Unquestionably one of the main British musical stars of her time, Alma Cogan died of cancer on 26th October 1966, when only 34.

Comedienne, film, stage and TV actress Dora Bryan was also an accomplished night-club performer and, early in the 1960s, a contracted singer with HMV. She recorded a number of show tunes as singles with Geoff's orchestra such as 'Diamonds are a Girl's Best Friend' and 'Little Girl from Little Rock' and then, later, an album entitled *My Name is Dora* (CLP 3596), singing more of the same. Numbers included 'Blue Room', 'There's A Small Hotel', 'I Love Being Here With You', 'Someone To Watch Over Me', 'Bill' (from *Showboat*) and 'The Party's Over'. Sharing the orchestral billing with Geoff were Tony Osborne and Alyn Ainsworth.

Well known for her weekly appearances on the late-night BBC television satirical show *That Was the Week That Was*, Millicent Martin recorded two numbers with Geoff and his orchestra, released as a single by Columbia in 1960 (DB 4466). The A side, 'Tintarella di Luna' had a positive Twist beat and the B side an upbeat standard, 'I Can Dream, Can't I?'

Producer Norman Newell first saw the pop duo Peter and Gordon in 1963 when they were appearing at London's newly-opened *Pickwick Club*. He immediately recognised their recording potential, soon signing them to a Columbia contract with Geoff as their musical director. Their first single, 'A World Without Love' (DB 7225), composed by John Lennon and Paul McCartney and released in March 1964, became a transatlantic hit topping the US charts and in the top twenty here for nine weeks. Many more followed, as well as several top-selling albums, some of which were reissued and all of them recorded with Geoff and his orchestra.

Meanwhile he continued his work in television and, in 1963, recorded music for the Granada TV series *Stories of Guy de Maupassant* and, with the Oldham Youth Choir, 'Song of Summer' for the BBC play *Yours for a Song*.

Celebrated for her saucy roles in the *Carry On* movies, Barbara Windsor received a 1963 BAFTA nomination as Best British film actress for her role in 'Sparrers Can't Sing'. Lionel Bart composed the title song and she recorded it with Geoff and his orchestra the same year; 'Sparrows', spelt correctly on the label. It was released by HMV (POP 1128) coupled with 'On Mother Kelly's Doorstep'. She was featured in 30 or more films, acted in almost 60 stage productions and for many years played the role of Peggy Mitchell in T.V.s *EastEnders*.

Tuesday 8 September, 1964 was a special occasion for everyone at Studio One, Abbey Road, when Marlene Dietrich arrived to record an album for HMV. Though the album sleeve fails to state the producer's name (it was surely Norman Newell) or provide orchestration information, EMI archive documents produce positive evidence that Geoff was the session's musical director. Issued as *Die Neue Marlene* (The New Marlene) CLP 1885, all 12 numbers were sung in German.

From the first time Norman Newell heard Johnny Mathis sing 'It's Not For Me To Say', recording the singer was always one of Newell's greatest ambitions. Contractual problems had proved a stumbling block until 1965, when HMV finally overcame them. Naturally most, if not all of their musical directors were anxious to be involved and though 14 songs were recorded, only two were performed with Geoff and his orchestra; Tony Osborne, Alyn Ainsworth and Allyn Ferguson provided the other accompaniments.

In his sleeve notes producer Norman Newell declares Johnny's rendering of 'Danny Boy' as the finest he'd ever heard, it being one of the two recorded with Geoff. The second, 'This is Love' was composed by Norman himself. The album was titled *Away From Home* (CLP 1926) and Geoff's contributions were soon also released as a single (HMV POP 1491), initially as a 'promo' and then for general release.

A year later, on 19 August, Johnny returned to Abbey Road to record two more songs with Geoff and his orchestra; 'The Impossible Dream' and 'Who Can I Say'. Confusion exists though, concerning the record's labelling details. Two different ones surfaced, one listing Geoff as the musical director, the other showing Glenn Osser in the same role. However, EMI Archives have provided studio matrix-card evidence which explicitly states that Geoff was the arranger and conductor on that recording session. Both discs were given the same number, HMV POP 1550, though neither displays the title 'Who Can I Say' on the B side. Instead, it is 'Hurry, It's Lovely Up Here', showing Glenn Osser as the conductor on both labels. To make matters worse, it has come to light that on playing both discs, it becomes evident that Geoff's orchestra is not on either of them.

Initially, the Abbey Road recording was put out by HMV as a demonstration 45rpm single on 2, September, 1966, numbered POP1550 and labelled 'Not For Sale'. This is the true recording, beginning with a military sound, whereas both the others open with violins, are identical orchestrations, even though one is credited to Geoff and the other to Glenn Osser.

Stanley Holloway, star of countless stage and screen productions and noted for his hilarious comic monologues, recorded an album for Columbia at Abbey Road with Geoff and his orchestra. Released in 1965 (33 SX 1656) called *Stanley, I Presume* and supported with the Lissa Gray Singers, the 12 numbers showcased more of his versatility, with 'Hello Dolly' opening the show. As well as 'Burlington Bertie' the album brings more trips down memory lane, including 'London Pride', 'I'm Old-Fashioned', 'As Time Goes By', 'The King's New Clothes' and 'That's Entertainment'.

Denis Lopez was not unknown to Geoff and Norman Newell when they worked together at Abbey Road Studios in 1967, for they had previously booked him countless times on albums with other artists. He was accepted as the most accomplished and authentic Latin-American multi-instrumentalist in the business and they organised a session to showcase his talents under his own name. He learned to play the saxophone during his schooldays and was a member of the RAF band during National Service. After demobilisation he developed a keen interest in Latin rhythms and soon took off for New York, the Caribbean and South America to study them from every possible aspect.

Geoff directed the accompaniment for this album, *The Mood Is Latin*, which was released on Studio 2 Stereo 155. Denis Lopez displays his remarkable talent with great effect on various sambas, boleros, mambos and smooth bossa novas and is backed by a combo playing vibes, flute, piano, bass and drums. The 12 tunes include Norman Newell's Oscar-nominated 'More' and Geoff's own composition, 'Katyna', a samba.

Noele Gordon, best known for her role as the motel proprietor in the TV soap opera *Crossroads*, recorded an album of 14 songs under Geoff's direction at Abbey Road in 1967. This was released in the Music for Pleasure series (MFP 50236 stereo). As was almost always the case, it was produced by Norman Newell and the outstanding titles included 'There's A Small Hotel', 'Mean To Me', 'Just One More Chance', 'These Foolish Things', 'The Best Things In Life Are Free', 'The Nearness Of You' and 'Somebody Loves Me'.

Columbia artist Des O'Connor also topped the hit parade with Geoff's orchestra. His single, 'I Pretend' (DB 8397) released in May, 1968, soared to No 1 and stayed in the charts for 36 weeks. The orchestral accompaniment on his 1968 Columbia début album, *Des O'Connor* (SCX 6208), was shared between Geoff's orchestra and that of Alyn Ainsworth. Numbers which Geoff arranged and directed were 'When You're Smiling', 'Red Roses For A Blue Lady', 'I'll Always Be In Love With You' and 'You Always Hurt The One You Love'.

Courtesy of Parlophone Records Limited

First Published 1968.

Courtesy Danny Williams

With 'Moon River' star Danny Williams at Abbey Road studios, c.1962.

Courtesy Danny Williams

Geoff high-stepping with Joy and Shirley Bassey at Danny Williams' 21st party.

Author's collection

British singing star Alma Cogan recorded a number of songs with Geoff and his orchestra, though died when only 34, on 26 October, 1966.

Courtesy Norman Newell

Coupled with her warm and engaging personality, Beryl Reid's career covered all aspects of showbusiness. She recorded more than a dozen songs with Geoff and his orchestra during the 1970s.

Courtesy Norman Newell

Marlene Dietrich, who recorded with Geoff and his orchestra at Abbey Road studios, Tuesday, 8th September, 1964.

Courtesy Norman Newell

Star of BBC TV's satirical *That Was The Week That Was*, Millicent Martin recorded at Abbey Road studios with Geoff and his orchestra in 1960.

Polishing an orchestration with his wife Joy, herself a capable pianist.

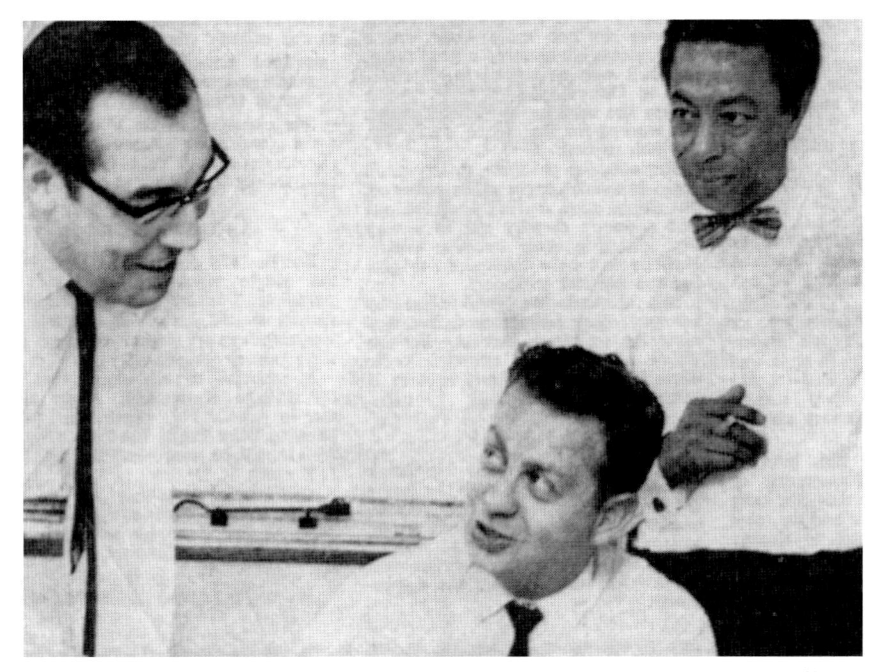

Mel Tormé, discussing his new LP with Norman Newell (left) and Geoff.

The tribal rock musical *Hair* that opened at the Shaftesbury Theatre, London, in September, 1968, was without question the most outrageous show-business event of the year, if not the decade. Nothing was left to the imagination – it covered just about everything – with the exception of the bodies of the actors – religion, drugs, sex, politics and every expletive imaginable. Needless to say, some audiences were shocked, even horrified. The music though was something else. Critics were unanimous with praise and first-nighter Norman Newell immediately decided to recreate the sound at Abbey Road studios with Geoff as the musical director. The recording took place on the first day of December, 1968, with Geoff's full orchestra and featured vocalists Dave Wintour and Pat Whitmore. It was released by Major Minor Records (SMCP 5004) and soon after in the United States by Pickwick Records (SCP 3169).

In 1968 Geoff assembled his orchestra at Abbey Road studios to record the music and songs from the successful West End production of "Bless the Bride" that had premiered at the Adelphi Theatre, London, in 1947. Surprisingly, though making a run of almost 900 performances, the show had never been recorded and Norman Newell believed it was long overdue. He decided to produce it as an LP in the Supertunes series on Music for Pleasure featuring Mary Millar and Roberto Cardinale in the starring roles and special guest, Peggy Mount. (MFP 1263).

Stirring memories of a romantic bygone era (1870) with music by Vivian Ellis and lyrics by H.P. Herbert the melodious tunes included 'Too Good To Be True', 'I've Never Been Kissed Before', 'Ma Belle Marguerite' and 'This Is My Lovely Day'.

Satirist Jake Thackray, who starred with Bernard Braden in TV shows for the BBC, was teamed with Geoff at EMI in 1969 to record an album for Columbia called *Jake's Progress* (SCX 6345). A top seller, and now a much sought-after collectors' item, it was soon followed by a second, *Bantam Cock* (SCX 6506). In both instances, the artist's own words and music were arranged and supervised by Geoff and played by Frank Horrox (piano), Ike Isaacs (guitar) and Frank Clarke (bass).

Ronnie Corbett, shortly before teaming up with Ronnie Barker for their first TV series, recorded with Geoff and his orchestra for the Philips label, produced by Norman Newell and accompanied by the Mike Sammes Singers. To test the waters, two titles were issued as a 45 'promo' for demonstration purposes only and not offered for sale. The songs were 'Its all going Up, Up, Up' as the A side and 'Put on a Happy Face', the other. Clearly it proved popular following D.J. airings, since it went out on general release in 1970 (numbered 6006 070).

American trumpet player Harry James, who shot to fame when only 20 after joining Benny Goodman's band in 1936, had become a highly successful bandleader with world acclaim long before he arrived at the Decca recording studios in London at the beginning of January, 1972. A glittering star with a string of hit records, he was about to record an album for the specialist Longines-Symphonette label.

The producer saw Geoff as the ideal musical director, and given the green light by EMI-Columbia with whom Geoff was exclusively contracted, signed him for the recording session. Propelled by drummer Kenny Clare, Geoff assembled a dynamic swing orchestra assembled from the best jazz and studio musicians in town and arranged most of the numbers himself. All ten were jazz-orientated standards such as 'Indiana', 'More Than You Know', 'And The Angels Sing', 'When It's Sleepy Time Down South', 'Don't Be That Way' and 'When The Saints Go Marchin' In'.

It went off without a hitch and was completed inside three days. Released on LP in 1972, (Longines-Symphonette LWS 766), a CD issue followed in the US in 1994 on Hindsight CD 702.

* * * * * *

In 1972 Norman Newell decided to record Neville Dickie, a boogie-woogie and stride piano specialist. Born in Durham in 1937 he took up the piano as a schoolboy and became a contestant on a Carroll Levis Talent Show. After two years National Service in the RAF he turned professional following a BBC Radio 2 audition and after an early chart success with 'Robin's Return' in 1969, played that year's summer season in Blackpool.

Geoff supplied rhythm accompaniment for this Norman Newell production, titled *Rags and Tatters* for the Supertunes series that was released by Contour Records, 2870 190. The album was hugely successful and a forerunner of things to come. The pianist's 1975 album *Back to Boogie* sold more than 100,000 copies and he proceeded to make dozens more and make personal appearances at festivals and on television both in this country and in the United States.

Early in 1973, producer Norman Newell recorded the first of four albums made with Geoff's orchestra using the same title as a novel he had read about the amorous exploits of a southern black slave called Mandingo on a plantation in Alabama, America, during the 1830's.

All eleven Afro/rock numbers on the first LP were given titles like 'Medicine Man', 'Black Fire', 'Fever Pitch' and 'Jungle Wedding' and, before the year was out, a second album was released. Though sales came nowhere near expectations and a third album (1974) and last (1977) were released. EMI still issued a compilation on *Music For Pleasure* ten years later (MFP 50428). Times change, tastes likewise and halfway through the 1990s all four *Mandingo* albums had become prized collectors' items changing hands for amazing sums. Now they are all available on compact disc, issued by EMI/Zonaphone 20965/20966.

Not forgetting his sister's tap-dancing expertise, Geoff devised some orchestrations and recorded them, with his sister Connie describing all the dance steps in a glossary on the record's sleeve. In 1973 he went to Butlin's Holiday Camp at Bognor Regis with *Opportunity Knocks* presenter Hughie Green where a sing-along album was recorded and once more produced and released by his EMI associate and great friend Norman Newell. Later, the producer teamed Geoff and his orchestra with Wayne King, an impressive young Australian concert pianist who earlier had been a contestant on Green's popular TV show.

Rochdale, as well as being the town where Geoff began his professional career, was the birthplace of Gracie Fields, the homespun happy-go-lucky lassie from Lancashire. Born Grace Stansfield on 9th January, 1898, it had to have been on the cards for them to make music together one day. It took longer than expected, but eventually Norman Newell brought them together and in 1974, at EMI's Studio Two, the tapes turned as Geoff raised his baton and Gracie sang 'Sally' as only she could. Together they recorded 14 songs synonymous with Gracie's distinguished career. The album *Gracie Fields – Superstar* (MFP 50052) included 'Little Old Lady', 'Getting to know You', 'Red Sails in the Sunset', 'The Isle of Capri' and naturally, 'Now is the Hour'. It must have been a memorable occasion, for after it was over Norman Newell wished that he had taped the hilarious banter that went on between them.

The following spring, he produced a second album, reuniting Gracie and Geoff at Chappells Studios in London during the third week of April. When released on the Warwick label as *The Golden Years of Gracie Fields,* it was presented in a glossy gatefold sleeve with 14 historic photographs and included more of her most popular songs, such as 'Pedro The Fisherman', 'The Biggest Aspidistra In The World', 'Christopher Robin Is Saying His Prayers', 'I'll See You Again' and 'Wish Me Luck (as you wave me goodbye)'. Gracie Fields, given the Freedom of Rochdale, died 27th September 1979 at the age of 81.

Syd Gillingham

"I look back on my ten years as EMI records' press officer as the happiest period of my working life. My job was to get publicity for our records and the artistes who made them - a task made so much easier if this or that person possessed a happy mix of talent and personality."

"Geoff fairly exuded both these qualities. And then some. His deep abiding love of, and outstanding talents for, the business of making glorious music, combined with a marvellous sense of humour and delightful, easy charm, made him one of the most popular interviewees with often hard-bitten hacks who over the years had seen other much less-gifted, so-called stars come and go. In short, Geoff was his own best publicist. A lovely man."

There were still many great years ahead when Geoff would chart courses to foreign parts, taking his marvellous talent to audiences as far as Australia and to the glitter and razzle-dazzle of Las Vegas. Before that though, he was asked to take his orchestra to a venue in London where he had never previously played. The personal invitation came from Prince Charles, the place was Buckingham Palace and the year was 1974.

Geoff had complete confidence in himself, took pride in his music and achieved great fame, though he never forgot for a moment what it had taken to get there. Dedication. He had it in spades. The more he put into life, the more successful he became. From his early childhood touring music halls, moving to different schoolrooms every week, his eagerness to learn the trombone, the world finally became his oyster. In his business, he proved himself a tour de force.

Geoff was immensely proud to have played at Buckingham Palace. The Prince's personal invitation was one of his most treasured possessions, with pride of place among his incredible collection of gold, silver and platinum records, collectively one short of 30. An invitation was later accepted to conduct the London Philharmonic Orchestra at the Royal Albert Hall and soon after, in September, 1981, he went to Moscow where he was interviewed on radio and invited to return for a series of concerts with his orchestra.

Courtesy Norman Newell

Control Room conference at E.M.I.'s Abbey Road studios, when Gracie Fields recorded 'Little Donkey' for Columbia. Pictured (right to left) are recording engineer Peter Bown, Gracie and husband Boris, recording manager Norman Newell, Teddie Holmes of Chappell & Co. music publishers, and musical director Geoff.

Author's collection

The Legendary Harry James
"Mr Trumpet"

The album was recorded at the studios of Decca Records (not related to the American Decca label) in London on January 6, 7 and 8, 1972, with the trumpeter fronting a band of England's finest jazz and studio musicians, supervised and conducted by Geoff. Several of the tracks feature a string section, reminiscent of some of Harry's most popular work of the '40s.

Superstar Johnny Mathis made two visits to Abbey Road to record with Geoff and his orchestra during the 60s.

Geoff Love collection

With Mrs Mills at a sing-a-long recording with Derek Bowden (bass), Bobby Kevin (drums) and Terry Walsh (guitar). c.1968.

Courtesy Ron Chapman

Conducting the London Philharmoic – Royal Albert Hall, 1981.

Geoff Love collection

In Red Square, Moscow, September, 1981, during a radio interview break, leading to an invitation to return for a series of orchestral concerts.

The Opera House at Sydney harbour in Australia is one of the modern world's most spectacular buildings. It was officially opened by the Queen in 1975 and not long afterwards Geoff was invited to conduct the Sydney Symphony Orchestra there for a series of promenade concerts in the spectacular concert hall which seats 2,700 people. All performances were sold out in advance.

Max Bygraves had no hesitation in asking Geoff to be his musical director for his Australian début in the mid 1970s. It was a huge success and they returned for several more appearances over subsequent years, the last time together during October, 1989.

In 1975 Geoff assembled his full orchestra at Chappell's Studios in London to record music by Michel Legrand and Ennio Morricone. Both were highly influential in the film world with many memorable compositions and film scores to their credit; Legrand, with 'Summer of 42', 'Lady Sings The Blues', 'The Thomas Crown Affair' etc. and several themes by Morricone for Sergio Leone's spaghetti westerns.

All these and very many more, were produced by Norman Newell and released during 1975 by EMI as a Double-Up twin album in stereo (DUO 118).

The same year Geoff flew to New York City to sign contracts for a Las Vegas début with Frank Ifield, another EMI artist. He stayed at the *Pennsylvania Hotel*, where most of the great American dance bands had played over the years and was said to have been taken completely by surprise when, upon phoning his wife Joy back home, he gave her the hotel's telephone number after glancing casually at the phone's dial. Yes, "Pennsylvania: Six, Five Thousand", one of Glenn Miller's famous tunes.

Frank Ifield opened in Las Vegas that autumn at the *International Hotel,* with Geoff directing an American orchestra playing his own arrangements. The show was so successful that they were promptly asked to appear as guests on the then National TV talk show being held in the hotel's casino. Then, a chance meeting with bandleader/recording maestro Quincy Jones led to an invitation to stop over in New York for a conducted sightseeing tour of the city's historic musical landmarks. Some time afterwards, Geoff made a second visit to Australia after GTV9 invited him to be a surprise guest on Frank Ifield's *This Is Your Life*.

The year was not without a major setback. On May 31, Geoff's mother, Frances, died of bronchopneumonia following a stroke at the age of 82. Her mother, Jane, had passed away at Walsden, near Todmorden, on 23 June 1949 aged 79; her father Johnson died younger still, aged 56, at Eastleigh, Hampshire, on 22 April, 1927.

In 1973, Todmorden's Old Brass Band decided to celebrate the 50th anniversary of its victory in *The People* Shield and Challenge Cup at the August 1923 Crystal Palace Championships. Geoff was approached to be guest conductor at a Town Hall concert to mark the occasion and while enthusiastic, his engagements prevented his attendance until the following year.

Present at the sell-out concert in 1974 were the following surviving members of the 1923 prizewinning band: Ashton Greenwood, Harry Turner, Harold Potentier, Gilbert Chatburn, Tom Sunderland, Sam Butterworth and "Wilty" Reynolds, who had approached Geoff initially. It was later decided to continue the concerts biannually with Geoff always returning to conduct the band right up until March 19 and 20,1988. He supported them twice in 1982, the second time in aid of a local flood appeal.

A little-known contretemps occurred when Geoff and Norman Newell recorded a tribute album to the Beatles at Chappell's New Bond Street studios in 1977. They wanted to issue the album in their Supertunes series on EMI's Music for Pleasure, but the Beatles' management refused to give permission for the group's name to be associated with a budget label. EMI got round the veto by pressing the album in Continental Europe where the Beatles' managers had no powers. The LP was pressed in France and duly made its appearance on French Music for Pleasure with the title *Les Plus Grands Titres des Beatles par Geoff Love et son orchestra* (MFP2M02699466).

EMI Archives have confirmed that they do not hold a copy or that the LP is even catalogued, stating that their collection consists only of records pressed in their Hayes, Middlesex factory.

In 1972, Geoff became active in the *Stars' Organisation for Spastics*, which had been founded in 1955. Two of its instigators, bandleader Cyril Stapleton and arranger Norrie Paramor, were good friends and they asked Geoff to team up with them on the orchestra side to play with the stars at charity concerts. There were many of them, stars and shows, and after conducting the inaugural Christmas carol concert at the Royal Festival Hall in 1973, he didn't miss another until conducting his last in 1990. He became a vice-president of the Stars' Organisation in 1980 and the same year was chosen by the British Film Academy as their musical director for that year's awards ceremony.

The following year, 1981, he helped form the *Young Persons Concert Foundation* with Bill Starling, Dame Vera Lynn and Sir Harry Secombe. This was a 60-strong orchestra of professional musicians between the ages of 18 and 25 selected from the country's foremost music colleges, who toured the country giving concerts to schoolchildren free of charge. The driving principle was that no child should be deprived of live music merely because they did not have access to it. Moreover, the aim was to improve young people's understanding of music by encouraging them to listen to and participate in music themslves.

The orchestra gave its first concert in November, 1982, at Highbury Grove School, Islington, north London, and its success thereafter attracted sponsorships from two of the country's leading banks and TV networks. The foundation's ambitous programme quickly brought requests from schools all over the country until the orchestra was giving upwards of 200 performances each year. It was only a matter of time before Geoff took the orchestra to his home town Todmorden where more than 800 children, from local schools to Calder High School, attended the hour-long concerts at the Town Hall, half of them between 11am and noon with remaining parties arriving for an afternoon performance at 2pm. Two days earlier the orchestra had performed in Huddersfield and, the day before, given two concerts for over 1,000 children in Middlesbrough.

Distance, though, was never an obstacle where a YPCF concert was concerned. For instance, in November, 1986, Geoff and the entire orchestra flew to Gibraltar giving four children's afternoon concerts and two evening concerts over five days. Geoff conducted the YPCF Orchestra for the last time on 9, May, 1990, at the North Bridge Leisure Centre, Halifax, West Yorkshire. Over 1500 schoolchildren packed the auditorium for a spring festival concert compered by TV personality Richard Whiteley in support of the Eureka Children's Museum.

Bill Starling

"My ex wife and I have very fond memories of Geoff and Joy, whom we first came to know around the late 1970s, when we used to walk our bassethound past their house, or they their dogs past our house. We lived within five minutes walk of each other."

"I first approached Geoff about my ideas for what subsequently became the Young Persons Concert Foundation in 1981 and, with his and Joy's enormous support, we managed to perform our first concerts in 1982 and the rest is history. We have, incidentally, performed for over half-a-million young people throughout the UK in the intervening years."

"On a personal note, Geoff and Joy were very supportive when my son (now 21) was taken into Great Ormond Street Hospital at the age of four for what could have turned out to be a life threatening condition. Fortunately, it proved otherwise but was nevertheless a very worrying period, especially as money was tight at the time. Geoff and Joy, understanding the situation, generously lent us their bungalow in Torre Dembarra for a fortnight, for which I shall always be indebted. We maintained close links with Torre, holidaying there regularly over a period of eight years or so while my son and daughter were growing up and I have extremely fond memories of our times there with Geoff and Joy (Joy and I particularly enjoyed Spanish red wine!),not forgetting the water-skiing which we all did and which Geoff introduced me to (and my kids), in 1984."

"I had the very great pleasure of knowing Geoff and Joy very well indeed between 1981 and 1991 and we counted them as among our closest friends, family really, as they acted as surrogate grandparents to our two children who only had one grandmother left after my own mother died in 1987. I still cherish the memories of our many good times together and feel privileged to have known such a generous and warm-hearted couple. I miss them greatly."

The interior of the majestic Sydney Opera House auditorium.

Author's collection

New York City, April, 1975, where Geoff signed contracts for his Las Vegas engagement with Frank Ifield.

Connie James collection

Geoff and Joy meet Quincy Jones in New York, late 1975.

FE 048955

CERTIFIED COPY 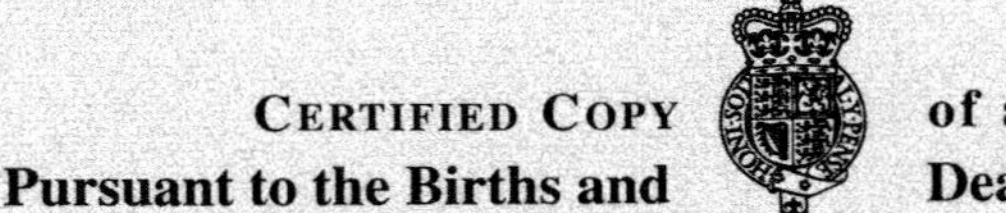 **of an ENTRY**

Pursuant to the Births and Deaths Registration Act 1953

Registration District Southampton

1927. **Death in the Sub-district of** Southampton Western **in the** County of Southampton

Columns:-	1	2	3	4	5	6	7	8	9
No.	When and where died	Name and surname	Sex	Age	Occupation	Cause of death	Signature, description and residence of informant	When registered	Signature of registrar
285	Twenty-Second April 1927 1a Chilworth Road U.D.	Johnson Ambler MAYCOCK	Male	56 years	of 102 Desborough Road Eastleigh U.D. an Actor	I a Carinoma of Stomach and Liver Certified by M.K. Jardine M.B.	Eleaner E. Evans Present at the death 182 Desborough Road Eastleigh Hants	Twenty Third April 1927	Sydney William Rolfe Registrar
285	Twenty Second April 1927. 1a Chilworth Road U.D.	Johnson Ambler Maycock	Male	56 years	182 Desborough Road Eastleigh U.D. an Actor	Carcinoma of Stomach and Liver Certified by M.K. Jardine M.B.	Eleaner E. Evans Present at the death 182 Desborough Road Eastleigh Hants	Twenty Third April 1927	Sydney William Rolfe Registrar

Certified to be a true copy of an entry in a register in my custody.

[signature] deputy Superintendent Registrar

14.09.2012 Date

Death certificate of Geoff's grandfather.

Todmorden Old Brass Band

CONCERT

Town Hall, Todmorden

SATURDAY, 27th APRIL, 1974

Guest Conductor: GEOFF LOVE

Conductor: ALAN POLLARD

Compere: JACK FOUNTAIN

Programme for Geoff's inaugural charity concert, 8 in total, from 1974-1988, at the Town Hall of his birthplace.

Courtesy Jeff Knowles

Conducting Todmorden Old Brass Band, Todmorden Town Hall, 27 April, 1974.

Courtesy Jeff Knowles

Conducting Todmorden Old Brass Band, Todmorden Town Hall, 27 April, 1974.

Geoff Love

conducts

'Music from the Movies'

13th, 14th, 15th November, 1986

at the

QUEEN'S CINEMA GIBRALTER

with the

Young Persons Concert Foundation
Symphony Orchestra

(Leader: Frederick August)

Gibraltar Chronicle

The Rock's Daily — First Published 1801

THE PAPER WITH NO POLITICAL BIAS.

THURSDAY, NOVEMBER 13, 1986. Vol CCLXVIII No. 55784 20p

Youth concert – a great success

Enthusiastically received by Gibraltar's schoolchildren the Young Persons Concert Foundation has proved a great success both in entertainment and musical education. World famous Geoff Love conducts and Gibraltarian violinist Freddie August leads the orchestra.

It's a day off today for the hardworking orchestra and their team who have brought their music to the Rock delighting their young audiences for free. Tomorrow and Saturday's performances at the Queen's Cinema are for the general public and the money obtained at the door will go towards financing further school concerts in England which will advertise Gibraltar's support.

Neither pop nor classical describe the music played by the orchestra composed of under 26 year olds who are just finding their feet in the professional world. The adult concerts will be music from the film world whilst the light music for the schools ranges from "The magnificent men in their flying machines" via Dvorak to "Star Wars". The little bit of classical that creeps in "was on the television sliced bread advert" smiles Geoff who is keen to introduce young people to good orchestral music. The jump from Boy George to Bartok needs to be bridged and YPCF does it.

Adrian Love, Geoff's son, a radio personality often heard on BFBS is the man behind the orchestra's visit to Gibraltar. He was overwhelmed with the support given to the visit by local businessmen and the community generally. He comperes the show.

Geoff has visited Gibraltar before, "one day some twenty years ago when the frontier was still open". One of Britain's music veterans — he leads the Manuel and Music of the Mountains group, arranges and composes particularly for television with themes such as "Bless this House" — and must be one of the quietest men in the entertainment business. His music is his voice.

"Before the war" he played trombone in his home town in Yorkshire and turned professional at the age of 17. He moved to the top of light music in the years that followed and calls himself a "middle of the road" music man.

The idea of a young orchestra for young people was Bill Starling's who is the ex-stationer turned full time orchestra administrator. His efforts and his neighbour's help (Geoff Love) drew the patronage and support from every corner of the music world — Adam Ant, Dame Kiri Te Kanawa, John Williams, Rolf Harris and many others.

The orchestra's Rock tour has been really special for Freddie August who returns to Gibraltar for the first time since he left in 1971. His mother of the Seruya family fell in love with her boss and, says, Freddie, "then came me".

He has visited his old home at Picton House much to the pleasure of his old neighbours and is surprised that although he left at the age of eight he remembers quite a few places. "Nothing will keep me from coming back again. It's a beautiful place".

Just having left Trinity College of Music Freddie now plays for the prestigious Halle Orchestra as well as freelancing for recording and studio work. His girlfriend, the orchestra's tympani player, has never seen him happier.

D.S.

Courtesy of Parlophone Records Limited

Now a genuine collector's item.
This album was pressed and issued in France owing to a serious contractual problem.

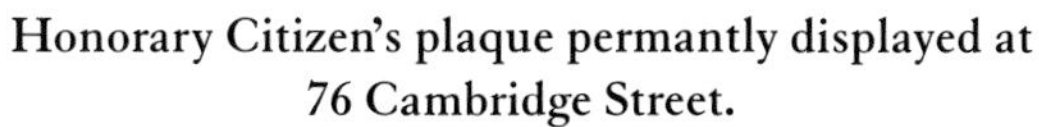
Honorary Citizen's plaque permantly displayed at 76 Cambridge Street.

During April, 1982, BBC Television cameras were in Todmorden, coinciding with one of Geoff's brass band concerts. The entertainer Roy Castle was presenting a series of six programmes for television called *The Brass Beat,* with the fifth subject being Geoff and his continuing links with his home town. Filmed over three days and screened on Friday, June 25, the programme brought footage of Geoff sitting in the Victorian bandstand at Centre Vale Park where over 50 years before he had presented the crown to his Rose Queen, talking about his early school life in Cambridge Street, learning to play the trombone, and getting started with bandleader Freddy Platt. The Brass Band was filmed in concert at the Town Hall over two nights, Saturday and Sunday, April 17 and 18, with Geoff conducting and Roy Castle soloing with the band on trumpet. Such was the demand for tickets, they were sold out two weeks in advance.

Out of sequence with the timing of his local band concerts, Geoff reappeared at Todmorden in 1985 to receive an honour of which he was immensely proud. Proposed by councillor and former town Mayor Dennis O'Neill for lifetime achievements and unstinting loyalty to his birthplace he was made an honorary citizen on May 18. Less than a year later, on March 20,1986, at the Odeon Theatre, Leicester Square, he was presented to the Queen at the year's Royal Film Performance. Just over two months later though he was driving north again, attending the funeral of bandleader Freddy Platt who had died on 31st May at the age of 74.

Geoff and his wife Joy were keen tennis players and in the mid 1960s they became members of the Mayfield Athletic Club in Palmers Green, London N13. It became special to them for weekend relaxation and they often attended Saturday-night dinner dances there with double-bass player and great friend Arthur Watts and his wife, Sylvia. The four were almost inseparable and it was not uncommon to see the party arrive with half a dozen more musicians and wives and then, during the resident band's interval, hit the stage themselves for some impromptu cabaret. Pearl Carr and Teddy Johnson sometimes joined them with a song or two for good measure, for as well as recording with Geoff at Columbia, they were close family friends.

Norman Newell and Geoff planning another recording with The Beverley Sisters

Courtesy *Halifax Courier*

With comperè Roy Castle at Todmorden Town Hall, Saturday, 18 April, 1982, preparing for BBC TV's *The Brass Beat.*

Geoff conducting the Todmorden Brass Band as Roy contemplates one of his many solo spots, 18 April, 1982.

Courtesy Harry Myers, Pic photos

Presented to the Queen at the Royal Film Performance, Odeon Theatre, Leicester Square, 20 March, 1986.

Courtesy Halifax Courier

Geoff conducts the Young Persons Concert Foundation for the last time, at Halifax, 9 May, 1990.

Courtesy Connie James

Geoff and Joy relaxing at their apartment at Torre Dembara, southern Spain.

18

Torre Dembarra is a small village on the Costa Dorada, a short distance east of Tarragona. Geoff loved Spain and owned an apartment in Torre' overlooking the sea where he and Joy spent much time enjoying their favourite pastime of water ski-ing. Moreover, its tranquillity became inspirational towards many of his music orchestrations, so his sojourns there were always called "working holidays".

Geoff had been suffering ill health well before his last visit to Torre' at the beginning of summer in 1991. His condition deteriorated during the first week of July, with Joy making arrangements to bring him home as quickly as possible. Once there, he was taken almost immediately to University College Hospital, London, where he died the next morning. It was Monday, July 8, 1991, just two months short of his 74th birthday.

His death from cancer was announced the world over with obituaries and tributes appearing in national newspapers, trade magazines and on radio and television. His hometown was mentioned in most of them, just as Geoff would have liked. His boyhood dream became reality and he never once lost his love of music, his constant search for perfection or his gift for working with the world's top entertainers. On his own tribute show, BBC presenter David Jacobs described Geoff as a very special human being and a fine musician whose records he had featured on programmes more times than he could remember. He introduced Max Bygraves, who called Geoff a brilliant musical director, kind and thoughtful and one of God's gentlemen. Orchestral conductor Ron Goodwin came forward with Norman Newell and Harry Gold to praise his musicianship, whileDennis King, recording star of the 60s King Brothers called Geoff an extraordinary musician and a warm dynamic man who so easily made you feel at home in awe-inspiring company. Bob Monkhouse said Geoff was full of dedication and determination yet extraordinarily kind with a unique sweetness of nature. As a colleague in the *Stars Organisation for Spastics,* he hastened to point out that Geoff conducted their inaugural Charity Christmas carol concert at the Royal Festival Hall in 1973 and never missed doing the same until he died.

Geoff's secretary, Dorothea Hillier (known to her friends and colleagues as Doff), was very close to her boss and his wife, Joy. They frequently met socially at the Mayfield Athletic Club in Palmers Green, North London, often joined there by Pearl Carr and Teddy Johnson, Norrie and Joan Paramor, Norman Newell, Glad' Mills and Peggy Mount.

Doff recalls: "The club had an annual dinner-dance at Firs Hall in Winchmore Hill, Enfield, where Geoff would have about 18 guests. During the evening he would take over the music for about an hour, singing with backing from the country's top musicians. I adored him – everyone did. He always took the same size in hats!"

I think we can presume that Doff was making clear that Geoff never became big-headed. She went on to say: "Geoff and Joy were the happiest and most contented couple I ever knew. I worked with them for 17 years, and the friendship and love between we three never changed, except to grow ever stronger. I could write a book on my life with the Loves".

Nor did Geoff forget his benefactor and mentor, Doctor John de Ville Mather. On 10th April, 1959, a carefully wrapped, bulky parcel was delivered to his home-town orchestra President, almost 30 years to the day since he funded the purchase of Geoff's first trombone. Inside its handsome case was a gleaming Boosey and Hawkes Imperial trombone and a letter of gratitude from Geoff with the message "I sincerely hope that this will give some kid the chance that you and Todmorden Orchestra gave to me".

Geoff and Joy had two children; Adrian, born 3 August, 1944, and Nigel, born 20 February, 1948. Adrian started a broadcasting career with a pirate radio station at the age of 22 and then secured a similar spot on the then BBC Light Programme. From there he went on air for Capitol Radio, increasing his popularity as a disc jockey before returning to the BBC on Radio 2 to present a weekly programme known as *Love in the Afternoon*. It proved highly successful and ran for a number of years until he switched to JAZZ FM and then to CLASSIC FM. Before his death on 10 March, 1999, aged 54, he had become a popular presenter for BBC local radio aired in southern counties. He was involved in a serious car accident many years before and suffered from frequent asthma attacks. He was married three times, with two daughters and one stepdaughter.

Nigel became a trained, fully qualified computer expert and was taken on by the major electrical company Belling within its computer division. He had been educated at the Grammar School in Tottenham where he became so keen and proficient at rugby that he was regularly selected to play for the Old Grammarians well after his school days were over. He moved to Manchester to take up a position with ICL (International Computers Limited) and soon met Diana Neville, whom he married in 1973. They had three sons, David, Peter and Michael, all of whom became competent at rugby; David often playing for Harlequin Amateurs. Nigel concluded his career as IT Consultant for the community dental services in Rochdale, Lancashire. He died on 14 October, 2013, aged 65, following a short illness. Joy, his mother had moved from London years before to live nearby, though at the age of 69 she succumbed to asthma and cardiac failure and died at Birch Hill Hospital, near Rochdale, on 8 June, 1993. Geoff's sister, Connie, who had put so much into her life, had remarried but lost her second husband, Derek, when he died on 6 May 2000. Connie passed away herself on 15 December, 2010, at the remarkable age of 96.

As well as being the foremost EMI/Columbia record producer during the 1950s and 1960s, Geoff's great friend Norman Newell was also a talented lyricist, credited with many top hits. His song 'More' (from the film Mondo Cane) was even nominated for an Oscar. Alma Cogan, Matt Monro and Shirley Bassey all made huge hits under his supervision, most of them with Geoff and his orchestra. His undoubted ability won him worldwide admiration and many of the industry's top awards, including a Grammy, an Emmy and a Golden Globe, as well as three Ivor Novello awards and six BMI awards. He was honoured with an OBE in 2004, prior to his death the same year, following an earlier stroke.

Geoff's contribution to showbusiness was immense. His records, and those in the *Manuel* series, sold worldwide and were so successful that many were re-pressed in the USA, Canada, Mexico, South America, Japan, Australia and France. Considering his tireless devotion to charity and his unwavering support of the Young Persons Concert Foundation, it is inexplicable that the Establishment never acknowledged it all. To someone so talented, who exuded such humility and held in such respect by his peers, an honour would have been justly deserved. In Shakespearian terms, there can be no doubt whatever, that there, stood a true star of England.

Courtesy Radio Times

Geoff with his son Adrian and part of his 29-piece display of gold and silver awards.

Courtesy Diana Love

All smiles. Relaxing with sons Nigel and Adrian, late-1980s.

Courtesy of Parlophone Records Limited

An exceptionally rare Japanese pressing of Geoff's best-selling movie themes.
First Published 1969.

Epilogue

There was a surprising occurrence during the book's final preparation, when an American citizen e-mailed the Todmorden Information Office from his home in the State of Michigan. He had found the online Halifax Courier / Todmorden News release about Geoff's 100-year celebrations, with the screening of his *This is Your Life* TV programme being of exceptional interest.

He introduced himself as Neil Zechman, an avid collector of Geoff's recordings, owning more than 150 LPs and/or CDs, adding that he had tried to secure a copy of this TV programme for very many years, without success. Furthermore that he wished to order a book, once it becomes available.

During 1983 he had corresponded with Geoff telling him about his collection and how he had bought much of it at a specialist record store in the city centre of Toronto, Canada, some three hours or so by car from his home near Detroit. It was much to Geoff's surprise when he learned that some had been pressed/issued in Canada, and, in a most cordial reply, thanked Neil for telling him so.

Subsequently, through a number of e-mails and phone conversations between us, Neil has not only sent a financial contribution towards the Centenary project, but, to his considerable delight, now has DVDs of both the *Life* and *Brass Beat* programmes. Moreover, his efforts in providing additional information with regard to Geoff's appearance with Frank Ifield in Las Vegas, were especially helpful.

ARTISTS GEOFF HAS WORKED WITH DURING HIS CAREER

Winifred Atwell
Shirley Bassey
Madeline Bell
Beverley Sisters
Lionel Blair
Dora Bryan
Max Bygraves
Roberto Cardinale
Pearl Carr
Carol Channing
Jeannie Carson
Roy Castle
Petula Clark
Rosemary Clooney
Russ Conway
Richard Clayderman
Alma Cogan
Ronnie Corbett
Billy Cotton
Bing Crosby
Randy Crawford
Five Dallas Boys
Tony Dalli
Deep River Boys
Neville Dickie
Marlene Dietrich
Ken Dodd
Adam Faith
Gracie Fields
Clinton Ford
Bruce Forsyth
Connie Francis
Judy Garland
Harry Gold
Noele Gordon
Hughie Green
Dickie Henderson
Vince Hill
Hinge and Brackett
Stanley Holloway
Frank Ifield
Harry James
Joni James
Pepe Jaramillo
Teddy Johnson
Dick Kallman
Howard Keel
King Brothers
Wayne King
Danny LaRue
Margaret Lockwood
Laurie London
Denis Lopez
Dennis Lotis
Vera Lynn
Fredye Marshall
Millicent Martin
Johnny Mathis
Don McKay
Mary Millar
Mrs Mills
Matt Monro
Helen O'Connell
Des O'Connor
Peter and Gordon
Peters Sisters
Bertice Reading
Beryl Reid
Roberta Rex
Shane Rimmer
Malcolm Robert
Paul Robeson
Marion Ryan
Jean Savage
Anne Shelton
Pauline Shepherd
Peter Skellern
The Spinners
Tommy Steele
Ricky Stevens
Dorothy Squires
Jimmy Tarbuck
Jake Thackray
Topol
Mel Tormé
Dickie Valentine
Frankie Vaughan
June Whitfield
Roger Whittaker
Danny Williams
Barbara Windsor
Norman Wisdom
Jimmy Young.

Moreover, in one form or another, Geoff participated in more than 60 albums in the "Music for Pleasure" series, each having at least 10 titles, all part and parcel of his undeniable legacy.

Coda

Geoff Love was born in Todmorden, Lancashire, on 4 September 1917, of an English mother and an American father. His only sister, Cornelia, played the violin in the town symphony orchestra and, contrary to reports that he had studied and played the instrument for two years, Geoff merely toyed with the idea, "stuck it for a few months", as he put it, and took up the trombone instead. What follows is a summary of his subsequent career in music.

1924 . . . . .joined a local boys choir - age 7.
1928 . . . . .took up the trombone - age 11.
1933 . . . . .joined Freddy Platt's Band at Rochdale - age 16.
1936 . . . . .joined Jan Ralfini's Touring Orchestra.
1939 . . . . .joined Alan Green's Show Band at Hastings Pier.
1940} . . . .Army Service. After initial training, helped to reform the King's Royal Rifles Band.
1946} Taught himself orchestration and wrote almost all of the KRRB band parts.
1946 . . . . .joined Harry Gold and his Pieces of Eight.
1947 . . . . .plays often on newly formed BBC radio Jazz Club broadcasts.
1950 . . . . .left Harry Gold. Took to freelance arranging for country's top dance bands, including Lew Stone, Eric Robinson, Stanley Black, Ted Heath, Billy Cotton, Ken Mackintosh and Cyril Stapleton. Also a staff arranger for Kasner Music Publishers. Played in the orchestras of Stone and Robinson – also with Harry Hines and Hal Evans.
1951 . . . . .Broadcasts with own orchestra on Radio Luxembourg with Alma Cogan, Anne Shelton, Dickie Valentine, Frankie Vaughan and Winifred Atwell. Also played at London's Astoria and two seasons at Regent Ballroom, Brighton.
1952 . . . . .Record industry growing rapidly. Joined Philips as musical director, launching its first British single with Johnny Brandon.
Also records with Oriole, Polydor and Polygon.
1954 . . . . .joined E.M.I. as musical director.
1955 . . . . .ITV opens. Geoff begins own weekly series same week. *On The Town*. 54-week run; originally planned for seven. Also accompanied Russ Conway and Dickie Valentine in their series.
1956} . . . .records continuously with multitude of stars.
1959} Cuts first own big band album *Heat Wave*.
1959 . . . . .First recording (7" single) as *Manuel and his Music of the Mountains*.
1959} . . . .Continues recording with many more stars and the first of 30 *Manuel* LP albums, a "bestkept" pseudonym.
1964 . . . . .Records at Abbey Road with Marlene Dietrich.
1965} . . . .Continues recording with more famous stars.
1968}

1968 ....Becomes musical director for first of four series of Max Bygraves TV shows (1973, 1978, 1979).

1969 .....Records 16 songs on Major Minor with vocalists Pat and Dave Wintour from the hit American Rock Musical "HAIR".

1969} ....As 1965/68

1970}

1972} ....Becomes active in *Stars Organisation for Spastics.*

1973} Conducts inaugural Christmas carol concert, Royal Festival Hall and does likewise for the next 16 years.

1973 ....Records first of four Afro/rock albums under pseudonym *Mandingo*.
Records with Hughie Green at Butlin's Holiday Camp, Bognor Regis.

1974 .....Becomes subject of TV's *This Is Your Life*.
Invited by Prince Charles to give orchestral concert at Buckingham Palace.

1974} ....Records 28 songs with Gracie Fields, issued on three LPs.

1975} Records album conducting London Philharmonic Orchestra.

1975 .....In concert with Frank Ifield – International Hotel, Las Vegas.

1976 .....Conducts Royal Philharmonic at Royal Albert Hall.
Conducts Sydney Symphony Orchestra at Sydney Opera House, Australia.

1976 .....Returns with Max Bygraves for Australian TV début.

1979 .....As *Manuel*, makes first ever digital recording at Abbey Road.

1980 .....Chosen by British Film Academy as MD for that year's awards ceremony.

1980 .....By now a number of his albums had been pressed and released in Australia, Japan, Mexico and the United States.

1981 .....Brainchild and co-founder of *Young Persons Concert Foundation.*

1982 .....(Nov) Conducted inaugural concert: Highbury Grove School, Islington, London.

1982 .....Subject of the BBC TV *The Brass Beat*. Filmed entirely in Todmorden. Number four of his six local brass band charity concerts there.

1985 .....Awarded Honorary Citizen of Todmorden.

1986 .....20 March. MD for Royal Film Performance, Leicester Square, London.

1986 .....Nov. Flies entire YPCF Orchestra to Gilbraltar for concerts.

1991 .....8 July, died University College Hospital, London, two months short of his 74th birthday.

* * * * * *

Geoff was an international icon, estimated to have recorded more than 4,000 titles, almost 1,500 of them, purely with his own orchestra. He was the proud owner of 15 gold discs, 13 silver discs, one platinum disc and a special trophy for the sale of 3 million albums.

British Phonograph Institute Awards (Platinum, Gold and Silver) had to conform to the following criteria:-

1. Only firm, invoiced sales to the trade, could qualify.
2. Only sales to the home trade and not export, could qualify.
3. Awards (appropriate discs) were only made to the record company (or label concerned) and to the artist, artist's manager and producer.

Awards were instituted and took effect from 1st April, 1973, and were not made for releases prior to that date.

Not for nothing then did Geoff deserve the showbusiness moniker
England's Mister Music